TOWARD CREATION
OF A NEW
WORLD
HISTORY

JAPAN LIBRARY

TOWARD CREATION OF A NEW WORLD HISTORY

HANEDA Masashi

TRANSLATED BY NODA Makito

Japan Publishing Industry Foundation for Culture

TRANSLATION NOTE

All Japanese names appearing in this book are written in the
Japanese order, with the family name first. In addition, all Japanese
words are romanized with the Hepburn system, and wherever
deemed appropriate, macrons have been applied to indicate long
vowels, except for the names of places, such as towns or prefectures,
and in the official romanized names of organizations, groups, and
associations in which macrons are not used.

Toward Creation of a New World History
By Haneda Masashi. Translated by Noda Makito.

Published by
Japan Publishing Industry Foundation for Culture (JPIC)
3-12-3 Kanda-Jinbocho, Chiyoda-ku, Tokyo 101-0051, Japan

First English edition: March 2018
© 2011 by Haneda Masashi
English translation © 2018 by Japan Publishing Industry Foundation
for Culture

Originally published in Japanese under the title *Atarashii sekaishi e*
by Iwanami Shoten in 2011.
English publishing rights arranged with Iwanami Shoten,
Publishers, Tokyo.

Jacket and cover design: Miki Kazuhiko, Ampersand Works

As this book is published primarily to be donated to overseas
universities, research institutions, public libraries and other
organizations, commercial publication rights are available. For all
enquiries regarding those rights, please contact the publisher of the
English edition at the following address: japanlibrary@jpic.or.jp

Printed in Japan
ISBN 978-4-86658-023-4
http://www.jpic.or.jp/japanlibrary/

CONTENTS

PREFACE TO THE ENGLISH EDITION

T HE ORIGINAL VERSION OF THE PRESENT VOLUME, *ATARASHII SEKAISHI E,* which was written in Japanese, was published in November 2011. In the years after that date until the writing of this preface in August 2017, I was blessed with a number of opportunities to undergo invaluable experiences and obtain new knowledge. I am particularly grateful to, first, a three-year series of tri-university symposiums on world history jointly organized with Benjamin Elman of the East Asian Studies Program of Princeton University and Ge Zhaoguang of the National Institute for Advanced Humanistic Studies, Fudan University, and, second, the Global History Collaborative project—which has carried out a variety of activities since its inception in 2014—with Jeremy Adelman of Princeton University, Alessandro Stanziani of École des Hautes Études en Sciences Sociales, Andreas Eckert of Humboldt-Universität zu Berlin, and Sebastian Conrad of Freie Universität Berlin. I have obtained countless new insights into methods and meanings of world history studies from these two projects. As a result, I have come to be convinced that some of the contents of the original book in Japanese need to be modified, although the basic argument still stands intact. Most of what I feel needs modifying is concerned with issues related to the positionality of historians and the audiences of their research results. Because this book is a translation of the original book written in Japanese, I do not think it appropriate to incorporate within the text the changes in my thinking that

I have experienced through the activities just mentioned. Instead, I have decided to take advantage of the opportunity to write a preface for the English version as a way to share with readers some of the points of note.

Because the original book was written in Japanese, only those who understand the language—most of whom are, of course, Japanese people—can read the original. Yet it can be said that the original book is also targeted at people in general, because it addresses the issues of people in general across nationalities and languages, in compliance with the basic rule of humanities, which claims to quest for universality. In other words, even though the actual reader of the original book is limited almost exclusively to the Japanese, the book includes narratives that appear to be addressed to people in general. Therefore, when the book says "we," it could mean both "we, the Japanese" and "we, the people on earth."

When I published the original version, I was not necessarily aware of these distinctions. I was not fully conscious of whether I was addressing issues that were limited to Japan and the Japanese or things that were common to people in general. If I were to write the book now, I would surely try to clarify whom I am talking about when I say "we." It was only recently, after I began having more frequent discussions with overseas historians, that I became more attentive to the positionality of researchers and the outcomes of their endeavors.

I would like to hastily add, though, that such cannot be my problem alone. I believe that positionality in historical studies is an issue which historians the world over should more earnestly keep in mind. For instance, even though English is a highly versatile language today, I dare say it does not liberate American historians from the problem of positionality. If an American historian talks mainly to American readers from the standpoint of an American, albeit unconsciously, then clearly positionality would be involved. When a non-American reader who can read English reads this author's sentence starting with "we," he/she may occasionally feel alienated or experience a sense that something is not quite right. Similarly, some readers of this book may have problems with some of its descriptions. I encourage these readers to once again look closely at whom I am talking to before dismissing the book.

Another positionality-related issue has also been on my mind lately. I have become increasingly convinced that people who aspire to study and portray a new world history such as the present volume proposes, particularly those who are historians, must clearly identify themselves as inhabitants of the earth. Unless they have a sense of belonging to the earth and think up methods for interpreting and describing a new world history on that basis, their works will not be able to awaken readers' sense of themselves as inhabitants of the earth. Some years have lapsed since the publication of the Japanese original of this book, and situations worldwide have become increasingly confusing. All the more reason, I would say, to hope that more and more people start behaving with an awareness of themselves as inhabitants of this earth, mutually transcending differences of views, so as to defend this one and only earth of ours and let people the world over live more peacefully and happily. I am convinced that the new world history that I am proposing can give a push, albeit a small one, to the flow toward this direction. This is so because it will be a historical study to create a new identity for all the people in the world.

Nevertheless, I wish to stress the following so as not to be misunderstood. I am by no means insisting that people everywhere identify themselves as inhabitants of the earth so that they all think and act identically. There are all kinds of people living in the world, having very diverse ideas. And people also have a sense of belonging to multiple groups of people simultaneously. While the majority of the Japanese people living in the Japanese archipelago speak the Japanese language and have a strong sense of belonging exclusively to Japan, the sense of belonging of, say, the Iraqi people is much more complicated than that. Aside from being Iraqi, they have language, religion, tribe and family, profession, habitat, and other clusters to which they feel a sense of belonging. Some of them are shared only by a portion of Iraqis dwelling in the Iraqi territory, while some others are shared across the national boundary. In the intensity of their sense of belonging to the state, the French are similar to the Japanese. And yet, for the French there is a larger cluster of Europe to which they feel a sense of belonging, while some of them feel a sense of belonging to such cross-territorial clusters as religions (Catholic, Protestant, Judaism, Islam, etc.) and languages (Basque and Alsatian aside from standard French).

To have a sense of belonging to the earth means that people the world over, who already have a sense of belonging to multiple groups of people, must add a new identity to their self-perception. Just as people who share the same identity, such as the Japanese, still have different views on other things among themselves, all the people with a sense of belonging to the earth do not necessarily possess identical values or views. Nor do they always act the same way. When numerous challenging problems on earth have to be solved, however, all people in the world must share this identity.

I must admit, here, that I had not thought it through when I used the term *"chikyū shimin"* instead of *"chikyū no jūmin"* in the original Japanese version. The English term that corresponds to *"chikyū shimin"* must be global citizen. But today I make it a rule to use *"chikyū no jūmin"* (inhabitant of the earth) instead of *"chikyū shimin"* (global citizen). The difference in the context between the Japanese and English languages makes it difficult to explain the reason for the choice of the former. Simply put, I have chosen an expression that is charged with fewer incidental meanings than "global," which has been contentious and divisive, and "citizen," which is normally associated with the modern Western context.

While I still very much believe in eliminating any specific group of people-centric historical view—and that spirit permeated the original Japanese version of the book—I believe it is only natural for the world history described in the Japanese language to contain a disproportionately large amount of information on Japan's past. The same can be said about China's past in the world history written in the Chinese language and Germany's past in the world history written in the German language. Extra caution must be paid, however, to ensure that country/region-centric perspectives and expressions do not sneak into the world history written in a specific language. A specific place-centric historical interpretation is completely different from a world history that contains a disproportionately large amount of information on a specific place. In any event, there can be more than one world history in this world. There should be countless world histories that can generate and reinforce people's identity as inhabitants of the earth, depending on the position-ality of their writers and readers. I wish to stress this point here.

I also would like to refer to the three methods that I introduced in the text as a means for realizing a new world history. I must admit they are radical proposals. I offer them as a way to break through the decades of stalemate in conventional world history interpretations and descriptions, which are nothing but a compilation of vertical histories of individual countries and regions bound together in a chronological order. This phenomenon has been particularly conspicuous in Japan. Today, seven years after the publication of the original Japanese version of this book, I no longer argue that vertical history is unnecessary. There should be peoples, countries, and regions that are in great need of their vertical histories now. To begin with, it is an impossibility to look back at one's past without presupposing chronological sequences.

Let us compare world history to a piece of fabric. While the chrono-logical sequence of time is the warp, my three proposals are the weft of the fabric. In contrast to the warp, which has already gone through ample tests of time, the weft is still untested. In order to complete a sturdy, beautiful piece of fabric, its warp must be mended where it is worn and its weft must be strengthened. When the weft is well woven into the fabric, we can expect a lovely new pattern to emerge.

It has been difficult so far to pay much attention to the weft for numer-ous reasons. One was the high level of interest in one-state historical studies and the histories of individual nations based on these studies, which made it unnecessary for historians to pay attention to the weft of history. Even when a historian became aware of the importance of the weft as an actual method of historical studies, it was difficult for a single historian to digest the contents of historical documents written in multiple languages. If a historian wished to comply with the basic rule of historical studies to attach weight to the reading of primary sources, he/she had to be austere about drawing a larger picture on the basis of outcomes from other historians. Because the big design of the picture was predetermined, historians had to concentrate on adding color to the details.

Nevertheless, the design of the picture has become antiquated after more than 100 years of drawing. It is time for it to be renewed. This being the case, individual historians should be permitted to draw a new picture, taking advantage of excellent research outcomes produced by other historians. Historians should also be allowed to collaborate with colleagues to ponder the design of the new picture. It is during this process that the three proposals that I made will prove to be an effective weft.

To draw a sketch of a specific era and to be conscious of horizontally connected histories is an undertaking closely related to the trend in historical studies called "global history." An important guidebook on this research method has been published recently by Sebastian Conrad, with whom I have conducted joint research and education programs through the Global History Collaborative initiative. Because I am in agreement with most of Conrad's arguments, I encourage readers who are interested in the current volume to read his book, too. Also, I contributed three articles (two in English and one in French) to two books and a periodical after publishing the Japanese original of the current volume. Seeing as they were written after 2011, their readers may discern the transition of my thinking. These articles and Conrad's book, as well as other principle works that appeared after the publication of the Japanese version, are listed in the Further Readings section following the Bibliography. They are closely related to the topics discussed in this book. Readers seeking further insight into topics discussed throughout this book will find that these sources provide a plethora of information.

I wish to inform readers that distinctive historical studies have also been conducted in non-English speaking countries for a long time, that these historical studies have come to interact more closely with their counterparts in other countries and regions as globalization advances rapidly, and that a new world historical interpretation based on the above global history method is called for in order to promote people's identity as inhabitants of the earth. It would be my utmost delight if through this book these messages are successfully conveyed to readers.

Haneda Masashi
August 2017

PREFACE TO THE JAPANESE EDITION

HIS IS A BOOK ABOUT WORLD HISTORY. READING THIS BOOK, HOWEVER, does not guarantee an understanding of the major flow of world history. Instead, this book aims to overturn the conventional common sense regarding world history as we know it. And it is my intention to propose the creation of a new, different world history.

The world history that we learn and understand today is already out of step with the times. Therefore, it is imperative to envisage a new world history that is suitable for our own time. Simply put, this is the message that I wish to convey to readers through this book. In order to accomplish this, let us first consider what kind of perception we have of world history and what is wrong with it. Subsequently, we will look into what is the new world history that is called for and how it can be created. The purpose of this book is not to discuss world history. It is to think, once again, about how to narrate the history of the world.

In recent years, whenever I am asked about my field of research, I make it a rule to explain that it is world history. Then, without exception, I am requested to specify the geographical area and the specific era I specialize in. When I reply by saying, "I am studying how to portray world history as a whole regardless of time and place," inquirers almost always look bewildered and murmur, "Ah, is that right," unable to keep up the conversation any longer. And this is only natural because my reply is highly unconventional in two ways.

In people's common sense, the major flow of world history and its portrayal have already been fixed. This is why, people believe, world history is taught in Japan as established knowledge in high school class-rooms. People also believe that a historian should have a specific region and era as his specialized area of research, to which he is supposed to dedicate his entire life to advance detailed and empirical studies, exhausting all the existing historical documents and related studies. Seen in this light, my reply goes against this common sense. Many may even wonder if I am really a historian. Unconventional as I might appear, however, I dare to declare that I am a specialist of world history, hoping people will realize that the understanding of world history which has long been taken for granted may not be the one and only understanding.

Skeptical of the way world history has been narrated and understood, I have been exploring for several years now how a new world history should be produced. This book is an interim report on my trial and error in this endeavor. I will be the first to admit that what I present here is by no means complete. Nevertheless, as I am repeatedly exposed to analyses, commentaries, and proposals on various contemporary incidents that quote the conventional understanding of world history uncritically, I am urged to take prompt action to remedy this situation. It is my sincere hope that this book inspires vigorous discussions on research methods as well as education and research systems of world history, which, in time, contribute to the emergence of a new world history and renewed perceptions of the world.

THE POWER OF HISTORY

ISTORY HAS POWER OF ITS OWN. IT HAS THE POWER TO CHANGE REALITY. It is also capable of directing people toward the future. One wonders, then, if this power can break through the sense of stagnation that has infested today's world and present visions of the future.

Some may be skeptical about the power of history, because history as we know it is essentially a narrative of days gone by. But history undoubtedly has such power. Recall, for instance, the historical view known as *kōkoku shikan* (the Japanese Empire-centered historical perspective based on state Shinto) that was prevalent in Japan before World War II. History textbooks in those days posited *Jinmu Tōsei* (the Eastern expedition of the sovereign Jinmu) as the beginning of the Empire of Japan, and the 2,600th anniversary of the founding of the empire was celebrated in 1940 accordingly. The majority of the Japanese people were made to believe that the Great Empire of Japan, which had been reigned over by an unbroken line of emperors, was an unparalleled existence. Led by leaders who were convinced that the Empire of Japan was mandated to construct a new order in East Asia, Japan rushed into the Second Sino-Japanese War and the Pacific War, only to be doomed.

Among intellectuals in the postwar period in Japan, after the total collapse of the *kōkoku shikan*, historians of the schools of modernism and Marxism became dominant figures. While those two schools were rivals that constantly denounced each other's respective interpretations of history, they nevertheless shared the view that Japan was Asiatic and, therefore, backwards compared to the western powers. In this sense, they can be likened to two rival sumo wrestlers on the same *dohyō*. Numerous writings by intellectuals of these two schools, based on the historical view that Japan was a backwards nation, had a decisive impact on postwar Japanese perceptions of the world and their own country's place in it. And this contributed to the formation of the basic framework and direction of Japanese society, for which it was imperative to catch up with the West.

To be sure, it is not only in Japan that history has the power to move a society and its people. A case in point is northwestern Europe in the nineteenth century. Today we take such narratives and frameworks for comprehension as German history and French history for granted. But it should be noted that they have not existed long, or remained unchanged over time. It was the works of nineteenth-century German and French historians such as Leopold von Ranke (1795–1886) and Jules Michelet (1798–1874) that introduced these narratives and frameworks. The state-centered "past" that these historians portrayed provided the foundation for the historical perception of the people (nation) who belonged to these states. And this historical perception, coupled with actual political moves and incidents, led to the gradual emergence of nation-states such as Germany and France. Subsequently, courses in history were established in state-run universities in Berlin and Paris; eventually, the Tokyo Imperial University (the present-day University of Tokyo) followed suit. These moves were in response to the need of newly founded states for national historical narratives that could per-suasively demonstrate to people the genesis and the founding ground of their nation-state. And these historical narratives were expected to nurture a sense of belonging among citizens.

These examples are surely convincing enough to demonstrate the power of history. History does have the power to modify realities and point people in the direction of a desirable future. Historical studies, a discipline to help people understand the present and foresee the future by studying days gone by, is, therefore, by no means a useless science.

On the contrary, it is a practical science that is closely connected to actual human communities. To be sure, it is not a discipline that can directly and immediately improve the lives of people like the science and technology that was responsible for the 634-meter-high Tokyo Sky Tree or the Internet. The interpretation of history provided by historical studies, nevertheless, can affect people's understanding of the world in a deeper, quieter, and more gradual way and, eventually, fundamentally alter the structure and the state of human society.

Dispirited Historical Studies

Unfortunately in today's Japan, historical studies and historians, which are both supposed to be sources of historical understanding, appear to be dispirited. After the turn of the century, a series of major incidents occurred one after another, shaking up Japan and the entire world. They include the September 11 attacks (9/11) in 2001, the Iraq War in 2003, the controversies among Japan, China, and South Korea surrounding Yasukuni Shrine that were triggered by Prime Minister Koizumi Jun'ichirō's visits to the shrine in 2006, as well as differences in historical perceptions among the three countries, and, in more recent years, Japan's territorial disputes with China and Korea over the Senkaku and Takeshima islands. The list shows that there have been numerous occasions in recent years for historians to offer much needed, proper commentaries and constructive proposals based on their own study as well as the latest findings in historical studies. Nonetheless, with only a few exceptions, we hardly witness historians actively engaged in these issues.

Compared to a few decades ago, it can be said that historians definitely have fewer chances to publish works that could affect overall trends of society. Unfortunately, it appears that discussions and narratives offered by contemporary Japanese historical studies are not equipped with the conceptual power to alter the reality or the attractiveness to point people towards a desirable future as they once did.

It appears, however, that this state of affairs is not attributable to people's loss of interest in the past. Suffice it to say that a great number of historical novels, ranging from those on ancient Rome to the Qing dynasty and modern Japan, have been in high demand. Some have even been televised. NHK (Japan Broadcasting Corporation) runs a yearlong historical, fictional drama series that remains highly popular among viewers despite ridicule from some that the shows are nothing more than home dramas staged in the past. Also, movies featuring historical figures are often produced to portray historical incidents. And in the world of video game software, historical games such as *Nobunaga's Ambition* and *Romance of the Three Kingdoms* seem to be generally in high demand. It is reported, too, that in Japan there has emerged a flock of young females called *rekijo* (female history lovers) who love to visit historical sites all over Japan. These anecdotes clearly show that people in Japan are very much interested in the past.

Given the above observations, I dare say it is only the discipline of historical studies and historians alone that appear to be dispirited. Why, then, are they in such an apathetic state? In my judgment, the answer to this question is by no means straightforward. In fact, the situation seems to be a result of the highly complicated entanglement of numerous factors. I submit that the most prominent of these factors is the emergence of a not-negligible gap between the history that ordinary people are looking for and the research results of historiographic specialists. In other words, although historians have not been lazy or negligent, their works have ceased to resonate with people.

As often pointed out, history is a question that people in today's world pose on the past. We need history to understand the present and decide where to go in the future. But the present becomes the past in the blink of an eye, and it changes constantly. Therefore, the questions posed on the past also naturally change as time goes by. From which angle one sees the past or what in the past is conceived to be important depends on the individual or group of individuals who pose the questions as well as the era when the questions are posed. Interpretation and understanding of the past is never constant nor unitary.

The *kōkoku shikan* of prewar Japan and the historical studies of postwar days were accepted and supported widely by many in their

respective eras. In revisiting the explanations offered by these historical perspectives today, however, one would experience a feeling that
something is wrong. That feeling comes from the realization that neither
view can persuasively explain why Japan and the world have come to be
what they are today—in other words, neither one presents a clear-cut
perspective on how Japan and the world reached their present state and
what their future prospects hold. Thus, as time moves on and society
changes, so does the past that people wish to reminisce, and so does
people's perception of the past. In other words, the history that people
desire changes and transforms as time goes by.

When a historical topic that suits the times is presented, it inspires
vigorous discussions among people, occasionally generating enough
energy to move an entire society. In Japan, in the period between the
end of World War II and the 1980s, for instance, there were several
occasions of such happy encounters between the times and history. This
being the case, it can be said that many contemporary historians have
failed to present historical images or materials that ordinary people are
interested in—in other words, that they can personally relate to.

It appears to me that, while time continues to advance, most historians are somehow stuck to positions they had taken for the past twenty
to thirty years. Meanwhile, historical studies continue to be increasingly
segmentalized, with historians producing treatises one after another that
nobody other than they would be interested to read. And it often happens
that research angles that once used to be highly important lose their
meaning in the contemporary world. When a research framework or a
particular topic that once appeared to be important does not match the
needs of an age anymore, no matter how much more in-depth research
is done, it would never attract the attention of the general public. Historians, therefore, need to have a clear self-awareness of the rationale
for their inquiries and the significance of their research topics in a contemporary context.

At the present time, there should be a specific perception of history
that our time calls for. When people start discussing the perception of
history earnestly as their own problem, contributing to the creation of a

new historical perception, this generates the power to overcome the past and move forward. What is required of historians today is not to faithfully obey the common sense of the discipline. Rather, historians must boldly propose a viewpoint of the past that is suitable to our own time.

The Power of a New World History

What, then, is the viewpoint of the past that people in our time should have? The answer to this question is a new world history. A world history is a basic intellectual tool that provides a foundation for viewing the world, for obtaining a well-balanced understanding of various incidents in today's globalized world, and for predicting the future direction of our societies.

Some may refute this, saying, world history already exists and we know world history because we learn it in high school. They would also say that, honestly speaking, history is hardly useful in real life. But I do not mean the world history as we think we know it today. I am referring to an unknown "world history of the global community" that we must create now. It is this "new world history" that should make us rediscover the power of history. This world history of the global community is perceived on the assumption that the world is one big community, and, therefore, it should provide us with a new sense of belonging as citizens in the global community.

It is obvious to anyone that today's world is an integrated unity. What happens in one region affects a faraway, unrelated region in the world and vice versa, creating a complicated pattern of interactions. Today, it is not possible to fully understand even the smallest incident anywhere in the world without paying attention to its implications on the rest of the world. For instance, subcultures and youth cultures among young Japanese today exert great influence on the tastes, fashion, and music of youth all over the world. It is said that many in France today think of manga, anime, or cosplay when they hear references to Japan. But it should be noted that these Japanese subcultures themselves are products of numerous influences from people all over the world.

The 2008 bankruptcy of Lehman Brothers sent a shockwave that spread across the globe, profoundly impacting the economies of many countries as it spread. The consequences of this reverberated back to the United States and shook up its politics and economy. The Internet has no boundary, while terrorists today are also engaged in cross-border activities. In fact, we only recently witnessed how political upheaval in Tunisia directly triggered political and societal turmoil in other Middle Eastern countries via the Internet (Arab Spring). Similarly, the devastating Fukushima nuclear accident in 2011 profoundly affected the outcome of two regional elections in Germany. Global warming is not a phenomenon that is caused by any single country or its people. It is an environmental problem caused by the total sum of people's behaviors all over the world.

It should be evident from these examples that the contemporary world has an integrated structure in which any movement or incident somewhere in the world will, without fail, have repercussions in other places. Therefore, in addressing the numerous challenges people are facing today in various places throughout the world, it is by no means adequate for a limited number of countries and their people to tackle these challenges on a national or group basis. It is imperative for all people in the world to be aware that they belong to one same global community and to act together hand in hand against these challenges from a global perspective. Once this global community is explicitly perceived as something that all people in the world belong to, the current problem of uncoordinated national responses to such global issues as environmental and natural resource problems, simultaneous world recessions, and nuclear power generation, would be greatly remedied. And the problem of postponing fundamental solutions to these issues would also be mitigated.

In actuality, however, it is not very often that people speak and act from the viewpoint of a global community. Even though the world economy has been significantly integrated and many common cultures have been shared globally, people still hold a strong sense of belonging to such limited groups or communities as nation-states or sovereign states, making them consider those groups' interests first. This is the main reason why people do not speak or act globally. People's awareness of being global citizens that live on the same planet is still low.

And this is why it is proactively important to conceive a new world history. This general perspective should be shared by all citizens of the earth. It is hoped that this new world history enhances people's sense of belonging as global citizens and helps construct the foundation of knowledge with which people can cope with all the challenges facing the world collaboratively. Hitherto, world history has been country-oriented, such as Japan's world history, Britain's world history, and Thailand's world history. Today, in addition to these national world histories, we must create a world history of the global community that meets the needs of our time. With the power of history that is generated by this new world history, we should be able to have better prospects for the future.

Structure of This Book

The central message of this book is as I've just explained: the world history that we know and learn about in schools is no longer appropriate for our time. We must create a new world history that meets the needs of our time.

This book delivers that central message in three parts. First, there exists a world history that we know and learn about in school. Second, this preexisting world history is no longer suitable for our time. And third, a new world history should be conceived. Corresponding to these three components, this book is made of the following four chapters.

Chapter 1 discusses the characteristics of world history as we know it today. How this particular version of world history became widely accepted in Japan is also explained. This chapter basically outlines how world history is understood in Japan today and traces how this understanding was established. It can be characterized as a history of world history, if you will. Readers only interested in the problems of the existing world history and what measures can be taken to alleviate those problems can actually skip this chapter and go straight to chapter 2.

Chapter 2 analyzes why world history as we know it is no longer appropriate for our time and where the greatest problem lies. Pointing out that three mutually interrelated points surrounding a Euro-centric historical view are the problems with the present perception of world history, this chapter proposes that the new world history should transcend these three points.

Chapters 3 and 4 take up conceptualization of a new world history. Chapter 3 introduces various attempts at formulating a new world history in the two major categories of (1) departing from the Euro-centric historical view, and (2) paying greater attention to commonalities and correlations. This chapter also tries to sort out what was effective and what was problematic in past attempts to formulate a new world history.

In chapter 4, I will attempt to outline what the new world history would be if I am to conceive it and how, specifically, I would try to accomplish it. This new world history is not yet before our eyes. It is something that has to be created anew. The concept that will be presented in this chapter is, therefore, by no means a completed or finished product. Nor does it mean that what I conceptualize in this chapter is the only effective path. It is my hope to inspire discussions about a new world history by offering my own working draft.

CHAPTER 1

TRACING THE HISTORY OF WORLD HISTORY

WORLD HISTORY IN CONTEMPORARY JAPAN

Various Understandings of World History

As this book begins, let us confirm how world history is generally understood in Japan today. How world history is understood and portrayed can vary significantly depending on where in Japan a person lives, what kind of life he/she has, what values he/she cherishes, and what he/she wishes to see in world history, among other factors. Thus, there should exist numerous types of world history.

As a matter of fact, hundreds of books with "world history" in their title have been published, and their contents vary widely. While some emphasize particular viewpoints on world history, including civilization networks, port towns, and maritime world history, others like to discuss goods or phenomena in the context of world history, such as the world history of sugar or epidemics. A wide variety of themes are discussed in the name of world history, including clothes, associations, national flags, counterfeit bills, espionage, and jealousy. Some themes are even bizarre like, for example, the world history of poisoning. Some books claim to be complete collections of world history, consisting of twenty or even thirty volumes. Anything goes, it appears, as far as world history is concerned.

Nevertheless, these widely divergent world history books all take for granted the existence of a particular type of world history as their premise—i.e., the framework for narration and the flow of world history as we learn it in high school. The contents of all of those apparently diverse world history books take for granted the existence of a standard world history in the sense that they are either objections to, complements or supplements to, additions of previously untouched topics to, or introductions of more detailed historical facts to the structure and descriptions of world history textbooks. Although it may appear that there exist numerous different world histories, the fact of the matter is these books simply reflect minor differences on the basis of a commonly shared broad framework and flow. What, then, is the basic structure of this standard world history like?

Education Ministry's Curriculum Guidelines

In Japan, the contents of all high school textbooks comply with curriculum guidelines compiled by the Ministry of Education, Culture, Sports, Science and Technology (MEXT). Even though there are several world history textbooks from different publishers, there hardly is any difference in the outlines of historical descriptions among them. This is because all of them comply with the education ministry's guidelines. In this sense, it can be said that the Japanese people's knowledge of world history has been influenced more by the education ministry's curriculum guidelines than by the textbooks themselves.

It was after the end of World War II that the Ministry of Education, Science and Culture (present-day MEXT) started compiling curriculum guidelines for high school textbooks. Since the first guideline published as a tentative proposal in 1947, a total of nine guidelines have been compiled as of today. In recent years, the guidelines have been revised every ten years or so, and the newest version was published in March 2009. Textbook publishers and writers are currently preparing new textbooks following the March 2009 revision of the curriculum guidelines.

Who compiles the MEXT's guidelines and how? Unfortunately, I do not know the details. The MEXT website reveals that university and high school teachers and members of school boards get together with officials in charge at the ministry to discuss the nearly completed draft curriculum guidelines at the working group of the Central Council for Education's Subdivision on Elementary and Lower Secondary Education. However, no information is available about the steps taken before this discussion. One can only conjecture that concerned parties produce the draft guidelines through mutual consultations.

At this point, let me introduce the newest curriculum guideline. At the outset, the guideline discusses the purpose of learning world history. The high school world history course is made of World History A for two credits and World History B for four credits. Each course has its own curriculum guideline issued by the MEXT, but let me quote the guideline for World History B, which sets out a more detailed purpose of learning. The guideline for World History A does not differ significantly from this.

> To have students understand the broad framework and evolution of the history of the world based on various sources and take into account geographic conditions and Japanese history, to have them study diversity and multiplicity of cultures and characteristics of the contemporary world from a broad perspective, to develop their ability to think historically and, thereby, to nurture their awareness and quality as Japanese citizens who live proactively in the international community.[*1]

It should be noted here that "Japanese history" is paired with "history of the world" and "Japanese citizens" with "the international community." From this, one can detect that the course on world history in Japan presupposes the existence of Japan, Japanese people, and Japanese history. What is required of Japanese students is their willingness to learn how Japan's own unique history is interconnected with the world's history.

It is obvious from this that the world history that the MEXT's curriculum guideline perceives is that for the Japanese people and not for anyone else. This is only natural because, after all, the guidelines are proposed by the Japanese government. In fact, as shown below, in instructions on specific contents to be taught, such expressions as "touch on Japanese history" and "relate it to Japanese history" are frequently used. Apparently, it is hoped that, by learning world history, students will gain a higher sense of belonging to their motherland of Japan.

Broad Framework of the History of the World

What is the "broad framework ... of the history of the world" that is set forth by the MEXT's guideline as a purpose for learning world history? Let us consider this question more concretely, along with the curriculum

---

*1   http://www.mext.go.jp/component/a_menu/education/micro_detail/__icsFiles/
afieldfile/2011/03/30/1304427_002.pdf (accessed on December 29, 2017).

guideline for World History B. As table 1 shows, the contents of the world history course are divided into five segments and themes, each with its own goals.

---

1. GATEWAY TO WORLD HISTORY

To identify appropriate themes concerning interactions between the natural environment and humankind, the connection between Japanese history and world history, and history in people's daily life; to stimulate students' interest in geography and history; and to have them realize the significance of studying world history through the studies of these themes.

2. FORMATION OF REGIONAL WORLDS

To have students understand that humankind adapted to local natural environments and constructed civilizations based on agriculture and pastoralism, which later provided foundations for larger regional worlds.

3. INTERACTIONS AMONG REGIONAL WORLDS AND REORGANIZATION

To have students understand that interactions among regional worlds became increasingly active with the development of maritime and inland networks in Eurasia as a background, which facilitated the formation of new regional worlds and their reorganization.

4. INTEGRATION OF REGIONAL WORLDS AND TRANSFORMATION

To have students understand that the integration of various regional worlds advanced as Asia prospered and Europe expanded. Students are also led to understand that the advancement of Europe into other regions, which by that time had consolidated the sovereign state system and accomplished industrialization, further promoted structuralization of the world and transformation of societies.

5. ARRIVAL OF A GLOBAL AGE

To have students understand how the advancement of science and technology and the remarkable expansion of production capabilities promoted the world's integration on a global scale and how interdependence among countries was further strengthened through two world wars and the cold war. Students are also led to consider challenges that humankind faces today from a historical perspective and look to the world in the twenty-first century.

SOURCE: http://www.mext.go.jp/component/a_menu/education/micro_detail/__icsFiles/afieldfile/2011/03/30/1304427_002.pdf (accessed on December 29, 2017).

Table 1. Contents of the MEXT's Curriculum Guideline for World History B

Except for the first segment, which is essentially confirmation of the purpose and significance of learning world history, the concrete contents to be taught in the second through fifth segments can be roughly summarized as follows: Multiple regional worlds with distinct characteristics had emerged in various locations in the world (but particularly in Eurasia), which in time developed mutual interactions and relations, leading to reorganization among them and transformation of the world. In the nineteenth century, the European world, which accomplished consolidation of nation-states and industrialization ahead of others, advanced into other regions around the globe, promoting structuralization of the world and social transformation in various places. In this way, the modern world was formed.

This is the broad framework of the history of the world as portrayed by the MEXT's curriculum guidelines. This framework is characterized by the ministry's grasp of the flow of world history as a process of the

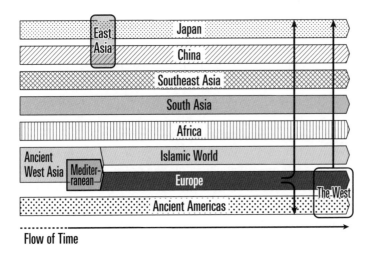

Flow of Time

Figure 1. World History as It Is Generally Understood in Japan Today

It is generally understood in Japan that numerous regional worlds that had originally existed separately gradually merged into a unified world by Europe's advance into various regions of the world since the sixteenth century.

emergence of several regional worlds, the interactions and reorganizations among them, and then their subsequent transformations and unification.

Figure 1 is a somewhat simplified illustration of this understanding of world history. In the MEXT's guidelines, the ancient Americas and Africa are not explicitly recognized as regional worlds. If one subscribes to a basic notion that there existed several distinct regional worlds on earth, this illustration serves its purpose without committing serious mistakes. Nonetheless, it must be pointed out that the relationship between the East Asian world and Japan is somewhat questionable. The MEXT's guidelines give an impression that Japan may be included in the East Asian world or it may not. And this is one of the weak points of not only the ministry's guidelines but, more importantly, of the current explanation of world history generally accepted in Japan.

Let Textbooks Talk

At their outset, Japanese world history textbooks often stress the significance of learning world history and give a summary of the flow of the history of the world. Thus, the opening section of a textbook should reveal the basic stance of the textbook writers toward world history. Let me quote here the summary section of two of representative textbooks. First:

To learn history, it is most important to understand the flow of a river called history, from a natural spring deep in the mountains to a brook and a river that pours into the ocean, setting aside minor details. This textbook divides this flow of history roughly into four parts. The first part describes how people adjusted to natural environments (climates), which were different from region to region, to survive, and how civilized worlds were formed in certain regions that were congenial to humankind. The second part describes how each of these civilized worlds strived to attain prosperity as if they were in competition. Section three discusses how development of inland and maritime traffic contributed to more extensive interactions among various civilized worlds, which often resulted in clashes among them. It also examines how a more powerful civilized world became dominant among peers, leading to unification of the world. The final section describes how unification led to unfortunate world wars and how everything that is happening in the world today has become a global issue today.[*2]

And second:

The starting point of our study of world history is our present time, when the world is a tight-knit body where developments in one region without failure affect other regions. This unitary world is a forum of complicated interactions among different societies with their own distinct cultures. And these societies are by no means under equal political and economic conditions. Examining the cause of the process that resulted in such a unification of the world, we find that it is the advancement of Europe into other regions since the late fifteenth century. One should next study the internal changes within European society that stimulated these advancements and the relations between European society and other regions that received these European advancements.

Why, then, did Europe have historical factors that led it to outward advancement, while other regions did not? To answer this question, one should look into the respective developments of each region prior to European advancements. The developments during this period were the very processes through which the foundations of regional worlds were formed.[*3]

The outlines of world history presented in these two textbooks are essentially the same. And both of them are based on the following, almost tacit assumptions: (1) the world is made of a number of different parts, each of which has its own history; and (2) of these different parts, the

---

*2 Ogata Isamu, et al., *Sekaishi B* [World history B] (Tokyo: Tokyo Shoseki, 2007), 3.
*3 Shibata Michio, et al., *Shinsekaishi* [New world history] (Tokyo: Yamakawa Shuppan, 2008), 3–4.

civilized world of Europe and states formed in this region became dominant over other parts, and they have substantially led the history of the world. On the basis of these assumptions, world history is understood as something like a bundle of histories of a number of different civilized worlds or states with respective chronological sequences bound together. And exchanges and interactions between and among civilized worlds/ states grew increasingly active as the time approached the present.

One should note that this view is essentially the same as the broad framework of history of the world of the MEXT's curriculum guidelines illustrated in figure 1. This shows that world history textbooks comply with the view on world history presented in the MEXT's curriculum guidelines.

In Japan today, it is usually believed that the world is made up of a number of mutually different countries and regions, where the West or Western countries lead others. And this worldview is in perfect concert with the outline of world history described by high school world history textbooks. This worldview and understanding of the history of the world becomes inextricably linked to our perception of the world.

When, then, was this view on the history of the world established? Did people in the Meiji era (1868–1912), for instance, understand world history in the same way as we do today? To begin with, when did the concept of world history and the way we grasp history become common? These questions will be addressed in the next section. The history of historical studies and history education dates back more than a century.

HISTORICAL PERCEPTION IN PREWAR JAPAN

Occidental History and National History

In Japan before World War II, it was a common practice to divide the entire world into three blocs and label their histories "national history," "Oriental history," and "Occidental history," respectively. History-related research and education were conducted along these three frameworks.

In those days, it was not considered realistic to study bygone days of the world in the framework of "world history." Although some junior high school textbooks at one time referred to world history, it never caught people's attention. Why, then, did the understanding of history in these three frameworks become common in Japan? Seeing as a number of books have already addressed this issue, let me only briefly explain the background and points to be noted.

In 1887, a new course called Historical Studies was opened in the College of Letters, Tokyo Imperial University. When the national university system was first adopted in the Meiji era in Japan, courses to be taught there and their contents were modeled after its counterparts in Western countries. To teach students in this new historical studies course, teachers were invited from Germany, which was considered to be an advanced country in history education. Ludwig Riess (1861–1928) joined the faculty at Tokyo Imperial University and introduced the historical perspectives and historical research methods that were taught in Germany in those days. The research method of empirical historical studies which Riess taught was that advocated by Leopold von Ranke, Riess' mentor. This method advocated "only to show what actually happened." Riess also taught the histories of European countries, including Germany, Britain, and France, which were products of this method. Such was the origin of a framework of historical understanding in Japan called "Occidental history." This framework is still valid today.

Here two things are worth noting. First, the course name at Tokyo Imperial University then was "historical studies" and not "Occidental history." This was a reflection of the historical perception prevalent in those days in northwest Europe that Japan during the Meiji era wished to pattern itself after. For intellectuals in northwest Europe, the world was divided into Europe and non-Europe. And from their perspective, historical studies was a science to trace the progress of human society. They believed that the only history that was worth studying was that of progressive Europe. Therefore, it is not surprising that Ranke's book, *Weltgeschichte: Die Römische Republik und ihre Weltherrschaft* (World history: The Roman Republic and its world rule) dealt only with Occidental history from the classic age through nineteenth-century Europe. What is called "Occidental history" in contemporary Japan is, thus, what was called the history of the world in northwest Europe in those days.

Second, it was mostly the political histories of European countries—advanced countries of the day in the region, such as Britain, France, and Germany, in particular—that Riess and, in later days, Japanese historians of Occidental history addressed, rather than the history of the European region as a whole or of the entire world. In those days, historians in European countries, which were in the midst of building nation-states, attached importance to the framework of the nation-state and believed it meaningful to study and interpret mainly political history within this framework. Riess, who had studied under Ranke, succeeded to this method and introduced it to Japan.

Taking into consideration the above two points, it was a truly epoch-making incident for Tokyo Imperial University to launch a course on national history (Japan's history) as early as 1889, only two years after the opening of the course in historical studies. In the common sense of intellectuals in northwest Europe in those days, there should not have been a history in Japan, seeing as Japan was a non-advancing, non-European country. To take up Japan's history in university, therefore, was nothing short of a challenge to this common understanding. Whether Japanese scholars who were involved in this decision were fully aware of this or not, it was, in the eyes of today's Japanese, the first challenge to the modern academic framework of Europe and the worldview as its premise.

From a different angle, however, it can be said that this start of a national history course was only a natural outcome. While teaching histories of advanced European countries in university was important for the Japanese government and intellectuals at the time, it must have been of the utmost importance for them to establish a state history of Japan as reigned over by the emperor. As a matter of fact, there already had been books on Japan's history, including, most notably, *Dai Nihonshi* (Great history of Japan), compiled by the Mito-*han* prior to the Meiji Restoration, as well as a compilation of an official history following the imperial rescript issued in 1869 after the Restoration. It shows that there already existed some kind of tradition of Japanese history in those days that was by no means a copy of the intellectual activities in European countries. Thus, it was not overly unnatural for a compilation of Japan's formal history to coexist with an attempt at compiling a history of Japan based on the empirical method of modern historical studies, because both shared a framework of state history. Since then, research and education on national history were pursued at Tokyo Imperial University without a break.

Establishment of Oriental History

The establishment of Oriental history as a framework of historical understanding significantly lagged behind that of Occidental history. It was as late as 1907 that a course on Oriental history was opened at Kyoto Imperial University; this was the very first course on Oriental history in a Japanese university. While a course on Chinese history had been opened at Tokyo Imperial University in 1904, it was not until 1910 that a course on Oriental history was established at that university on the basis of this Chinese history course.

At the secondary education level, in contrast, the concept of Oriental history and the foundation for its teaching had already been prepared ahead of university education. In fact, a perception of history in the name of Oriental history had already been advocated in 1894 by the historian Naka Michiyo (1851–1908), while, in 1898, a secondary school textbook on Oriental history compiled by Kuwabara Jitsuzō (1871–1931) was published. According to contemporary writer Kubodera Kōichi (1942–), although the term Oriental history had already been used a few times before Naka used it, it was Naka's original idea to position Oriental history as a part of the history of the entire world and set it up as a framework for historiographic study.[*4]

---

*4   Kubodera Kōichi, *Tōyōgaku kotohajime: Naka Michiyo to sono jidai* [Beginning of oriental studies: Naka Michiyo and his time] (Tokyo: Heibonsha, 2009).

The emergence of a uniquely Japanese perception of Oriental history had the effect of making the concept of an Occidental history clearer as the other half of a pair. The world history studied in northwest Europe became the "Occidental history" in Japan. Thus, in Japan toward the end of the nineteenth century, Occidental history as well as Oriental history were taught in secondary schools along with the national history.

Miyazaki Ichisada, a leading authority of Oriental history in postwar Japan, has the following to say about the emergence of Oriental history as a framework for historical understanding:

As the national awareness of the Japanese heightened, Japanese historians found it increasingly uncomfortable to view the history of East Asia as Chinese history or a history of the Chinese people. This led to the formation of the Oriental history. The most prominent among the founding fathers of Oriental history was Dr. Kuwabara Jitsuzō, whose *Chūtō tōyōshi* (Middle school textbook on Oriental history) was much more than a mere school textbook. This book was an academic classic that set an example for the discipline of Oriental history over years and decades.[*5]

When there already had existed the frameworks of the Occidental history and national history (history of Japan), it was, academically speaking, natural for Oriental history as a historical view to be conceived, covering the area between the Occident, Europe in particular, and Japan with special attention to China and its neighboring countries. In order for a course on a new discipline to be opened in a national university, however, pure academic reasoning should not have been enough.

This should be obvious when one considers the timing of the openings of the Oriental history courses at imperial universities in Tokyo and Kyoto. Their openings perfectly coincided with Japan's victory in

---

[*5] Miyazaki Ichisada, foreword to *Ajia rekishi kenkyū nyūmon, dai 1-kan* [Introduction to Asian historiographical studies, vol. 1], ed. Shimada Kenji (Kyoto: Dohosha Shuppan, 1983).

the Russo-Japanese War, when Japan obtained a foothold for advance-
ment into Mainland China via the Korean Peninsula. According to *Kyoto Daigaku Bungakubu 50-nenshi* (50-year history of the Faculty of Letters, Kyoto University), "Our College of Letters was founded in the 39th Year of Meiji (1906), one year after the victory in the Russo-Japanese War, when the Japanese people's attention was focused on Asia as a whole. Therefore, it was truly appropriate for our university to place emphasis on the Oriental studies from its founding years." But Miyazaki Ichisada praised the opening of the Oriental history course in an even more straightforward manner, saying, "It can be said that this discipline called Oriental history was born with the mission to help Japan realize the ideal of taking leadership in defending Asia against invasions of the Western powers."[*6]

Thus, Oriental history as a framework for historical understanding was established as a kind of practical science based on such very realistic demands.

Histories Divided into Three

At this point, three divisions of history were firmly established, i.e., the history of Japan, Oriental history, and Occidental history. This uniquely Japanese arrangement has continued through to the present. These three divisions were by no means made as an outcome of purely academic pursuit. Portraying and learning each of these three divisions had a very important significance in real-life society. The purpose of national history (history of Japan) was to firmly establish the notion of "Japan, our own nation-state"; the purpose of Occidental history was to show Japan a model it should aspire to follow and catch up to; and the purpose of the history of the Orient (Oriental history) was to make Japanese people understand the history of Oriental countries of which Japan should take the leadership role in resisting domination by the West.

[*6] Miyazaki Ichisada, afterword to *Miyazaki Ichisada zenshū 2: Tōyōshi* [Complete works of Miyazaki Ichisada 2: Oriental history] (Tokyo: Iwanami Shoten, 1992).

By learning the histories of these three divisions, Japanese people were able to consolidate their perception of the world. Thus, frameworks for historical narration and people's perceptions of the world were solidly in synch in Japan in those days.

Because the education of and research of history continued to be conducted along these three divisions in universities, as well as in secondary schools until the end of World War II, people in Japan hardly had a chance to become conscious of world history, a superstructure over those three divisions. Even when some became conscious of world history, it must have been perceived as a mixed bag of three different histories of the advanced West, the backward Orient, and Japan that was meant to lead Oriental countries to counter the West. It is safe enough to think that it was after Japan's defeat in World War II in 1945 that the Japanese people began to find substantial meaning in the concept of world history.

BIRTH OF WORLD HISTORY

Establishment of World History as a High School Course

It was in 1947 that the Ministry of Education, Science and Culture published the first curriculum guideline—albeit as a tentative proposal. The publishing of the guideline was probably driven by the realization that, it being two years since defeat in World War II, when everything had to be restarted from scratch, Japan needed a new guideline for its primary and secondary education. It should be noted that this tentative curriculum guideline did not include world history. History-related subjects included in the high school curriculum under the new system of education were limited to Oriental history and Occidental history. It was stipulated that national history (the history of Japan) be taught in social studies classes, together with politics and economics. In those days, Japan was under occupation by the Allied forces; therefore, the teaching of national history was prohibited, even if it was a new interpretation of Japan's history that was different from prewar national history.

Oriental history and Occidental history were the names of the courses taught in prewar history classes. Thus, it can be said that, in 1947, the tendency to divide the world into the Eastern and the Western worlds to understand world history was still intact as in prewar days. But the major difference from the prewar days was that, in the proposed curriculum, Japan was deprived of its special position and, instead, incorporated in the East. The section on Occidental history in the first guideline of the Ministry of Education, Science and Culture reads:

While the history of humankind as a whole has shown a certain integrated progress as a unity, the progress of individual regions has differed from area to area. And this is why world history is divided into Oriental and Occidental histories. Oriental history is important for us in order to understand the uniqueness of the East, of which Japan forms an integral part. Because Western civilization is the mainstream of today's world, however, knowledge of Occidental history is absolutely essential even to understand the history of the East.

In the statement that Japan is an integral part of the East, one can detect the worldview of the author who wrote this paragraph immediately after Japan's defeat in the war.

It was not until 1951, when the second curriculum guideline was published four years after the first, that a course on world history was included. In that second guideline, the course on world history appeared as a course to replace Oriental history and Occidental history. To be more precise, the Ministry of Education, Science and Culture had proposed world history as a high school course three years earlier in its 1948 notification concerning the reform of courses to be taught in high school under the new education system.

The background to the opening of a new course in world history was not necessarily well spelled out. Some say that the decision to open a new course was made without the participation of historians so as to comply with a suggestion from the Civil Information and Education Section of the occupation forces. However, it is also true that a number of Japanese historians had explored a new direction in history research since immediately after the war, earnestly reflecting on the way historical studies, particularly those on national history, had been conducted in prewar days. The Historical Science Society of Japan, for instance, published its report at the 1949 convention under the title *Sekaishi no kihon hōsoku* (Fundamental laws of world history), which discussed fervently how to perceive Asia and Japan in world history from the perspective of Marxism.

Nevertheless, it is obvious that university historians did not actively take the initiative in establishing a course on world history. In fact, major universities in Japan, including the University of Tokyo and Kyoto University, even today—more than sixty some years after the war—still hang on to the prewar framework of history research and education composed of Oriental and Occidental histories. Thus, while in universities, education and research on history have continued to be conducted under the old framework, high school education began to use a new framework of world history since 1951. Inevitably, a subtle gap emerged between the two. Although space does not allow me to pursue this issue any further, the negative effect of the absence of systematic education and research on world history in universities has been grave. Ordinarily, it is the graduates of a university's department of history who become high school teachers of social studies. Novice teachers, who have not been given training in world history, have no other choice than to come up with their own method of teaching world history through trial and error.

Western-Centric World History

In the education ministry's curriculum guideline of 1951, when the world history course was first introduced, the actual contents to be taught were divided into three sections: pre-modern society, modern society, and contemporary society. Each section was further divided into more detailed subsections. At the risk of boring readers, these sections and subsections are summarized in table 2.

PRE-MODERN SOCIETY

1. Development of Primitive Society

a. Advent of Humankind
b. Development of Primitive Living
c. Nature of Primitive Religions
d. Ethnic Systems
e. Emergence of Civilizations

2. Formation of Ancient States

a. Unification of Ancient Orient
b. Greek Polis
c. World Empire of Rome
d. Unified State of India
e. Unified China
f. Ancient State in Japan

3. Ancient Cultures and Their Characteristics

a. Development of Letters and Their Diffusion
b. Improvement of the Art of Living
c. Nature of Ancient Arts
d. Ancient Legal Systems and Social Organization
e. Ancient Thoughts and Learnings

4. Formation and Development of Feudal Societies in the Occident

a. Great Migration and Formation of Kingdoms
b. Development of Large Land Ownership System and Establishment of Class Systems
c. Expansion of Church's Power
d. Characteristics of Medieval Cultures
e. Development of Medieval Cities
f. Fall of Feudal Nobles

5. Changes of Authoritarian States in Asia

a. Rise and Fall of Dynasties
b. Rise of Warrior Politics
c. Establishment of Bureaucratic System in China
d. Changes of Cultural Contents
e. Development of Social Economy
f. Rebellions of Peasants
g. Fall of Authoritarian Politics
h. Characteristics of Feudal System in Japan

6. Contacts and Exchanges between Ethnic Groups and Cultures

a. Hellenism
b. Silk Road
c. Crusades
d. Westward Diffusion of Eastern Cultures
e. Sino-Japanese Cultural Exchanges
f. Conquest Dynasties

7. Religion and Culture of Everyday Life

a. Development of Christianity
b. Expansion of Islam
c. Spread of Buddhism
d. Characteristics of Hindu Religion
e. Daoism and Folk Beliefs

MODERN SOCIETY

1. Rise of the Bourgeoisie and Its Influences

a. Renaissance
b. Reformation
c. Geographical Discovery
d. Development of Commercial Capital
e. Scientific Development

2. Absolute Monarchy and Bourgeois Revolution

a. Emergence of Absolute Monarchy
b. Establishment of Overseas Colonies

Table 2. Ministry of Education, Science and Culture's Curriculum Guideline (1951)

c. English Revolutions
d. The Enlightenment
e. Independence of the United States
f. French Revolution

3. **Industrial Revolution and Its Impact**
   a. Industrial Revolution in Britain
   b. Development of Modern Cities
   c. Development of Means of Transportation
   d. Development of Industrial Capital
   e. Rise of Labor Problems
   f. Improvement of Daily Life

4. **Modern Democracy and Its Development**
   a. Development of British Parliamentary Politics
   b. Establishment of French Republic
   c. Development of Nationalism
   d. Civil War in the United States

5. **European Powers' Advancement into the World**
   a. Rise of Imperialism
   b. Balance of Power among Major Powers
   c. Scramble for Africa
   d. Asian Policies of Powers

6. **Asia's Modernization**
   a. Taiping Rebellion
   b. Fall of Qing dynasty and Xinhai Revolution
   c. Indian National Congress and Independence Movement in India
   d. Meiji Restoration

7. **Development of Modern Cultures**
   a. Modern Thought and Their Nature
   b. Diversification of Academic Pursuit
   c. Development of Natural Sciences
   d. Spread of Public Education
   e. Improvement of Living Standard

CONTEMPORARY SOCIETY

1. **World War I and Signing of the Treaty of Versailles**
   a. Progress of World War I
   b. Russian Revolution
   c. League of Nations
   d. International Cooperation

2. **Totalitarianism and World War II**
   a. The Great Depression
   b. Rise of the United States
   c. Solid Development of the Soviet Union
   d. Japan's Advancement into Mainland China
   e. Rise of Totalitarian States
   f. Eruption of World War II and Its Progress

3. **Post–WWII World Situation**
   a. United Nations and the World Peace Movement
   b. Advancement of the United States and the Soviet Union
   c. Nationalism Movements in Asia
   d. Dominance of American Economy
   e. Nature of Contemporary Cultures

4. **Place of Contemporary Japan in World History**
   a. Japan's Democratization
   b. Japan's International Status
   c. Construction of Japan's Culture

SOURCE: https://www.nier.go.jp/guideline/s26jhs3/chap2.htm (accessed on December 29, 2017).

Some interesting observations can be made about this table of contents. First, the entire course is divided into three chronological periods, as previously mentioned: pre-modern, modern, and contemporary. While today the pre-modern period is usually further divided into the ancient, medieval, and early modern periods, the first curriculum guideline for the world history course did not adopt this subdivision. As a result, the demarcation between modern society and pre-modern society became all the more meaningful, inevitably further emphasizing the importance of the modern time.

The second interesting observation is that the whole curriculum was constructed around the two pillars of the West (Europe) and the East (Asia). Particularly, in the first two sections (pre-modern and modern societies), a broad framework of historic space dichotomized into the West and the East, or Europe and Asia, was deliberately used. Over the first fifty years of the twentieth century until publication of this curriculum guideline, the history of the world was perceived and narrated on the premise of this dichotomized historical space. Therefore, when those who authored the guideline were suddenly asked to construct a world history curriculum, they must have thought of no other effective method than resorting to this half-century-old framework.

Third, it is interesting that there was a noticeable imbalance between Western history and Eastern history with regards to the number of themes to be taught. This was particularly remarkable in the modern society period. While an almost equal number of themes were allotted to Europe and Asia in the pre-modern society period, the first five of seven major themes in the second period of the modern society category were concerned with Europe. In other words, topics in this period were arranged such that students would learn about modern Europe in detail first, followed by a theme on modernization in Asia. This sequence must have been based on the writers' understanding that modernization in Asia had taken place under the influence of European modernization. Taking into consideration that development of modern cultures, the seventh and last topic for modern society, was essentially an explanation of modern cultures in Europe, it can be said that this second period (i.e., modern society) was almost entirely about modern Europe. It also should be noted that only passing reference was made to the United States, and it was positioned as if it were incorporated in European history.

From this list of contents, one can detect that the flow of world history was interpreted in Japan in those days as modernization initiated and led by Europe (or the Western world), followed by Asia under European influence, thus consequently leading to unification of the entire world. It is a world history centered on an axis of Occidental history. And this view finds an echo in the section for Oriental history of the 1947 curriculum guideline, which read, "Because the modern culture of the West was a superior culture, it was only natural for the antiquated culture of the East to be overwhelmed by it. Thus, the world became united, in which the East devoted itself to learning and digesting the superior culture of the West."[*7]

Aside from the above basic framework, which had been carried over from prewar days, there was another factor behind the content of the curriculum guideline. Immediately after World War II, education ministry officials were forced to explore how to teach world history, which was abruptly added to the high school curriculum, without the benefit of models to follow. The reference to unification of the Occidental and Oriental histories and the supremacy of the modern culture of Europe was the result of this exploration. It can be said that this guideline accurately reflected political and social conditions in those days as well as the Japanese people's world perception.

The education ministry published its second curriculum guideline that included world history in 1956. This guideline succeeded the dichotomic framework of the first guideline—that is, the West vs. the East, or Europe vs. Asia. At the end of this second guideline were "three points to note," which included the statement, "While there may be many other ways to combine the East and the West, it is not desirable,

---

*7 https://www.nier.go.jp/guideline/s22ejs3/chap1.htm (accessed on December 29, 2017).

from the viewpoint of the purpose of the course, to treat Oriental and Occidental histories separately, and merely provide students with separate knowledge on them."*8 This statement might have been provoked by the education on and research of history in universities, which were still considering history in the three parts of the history of Japan and the Oriental and Occidental histories. This statement seemed to deliberately stress that high school world history courses should not be patterned after this university model.

Themes in this second curriculum guideline included such terms as "ethnic groups in Asia" and "authoritarian states in Asia," hinting at the Japanese officials' inclination to lump Asian countries into a group. Inevitably, therefore, the presence of more than one cultural sphere was not envisioned in Asia.

Subsequent Curriculum Guidelines

The education ministry's curriculum guideline subsequently underwent five revisions. The newest one was published in 2009. If one compared the contents of all of the past guidelines, meticulously tracing all the changes, a number of interesting points for discussion would be revealed. Because this comparison would digress from the main theme of this book, however, let me confine myself to a brief summary of the characteristics of past curriculum guidelines, focusing only on their basic stance toward how to understand the flow of world history.

The 1960 version contained the following annotation for the first time: "It is conceivable to have students learn the histories of different regions of the world through a cultural sphere, such as Europe, India/West Asia, and East Asia, during the period when individual regions had not yet been closely related to each other, such as the period of ancient to medieval times in Europe."*9

From the 1970 version on, the term "cultural sphere" (e.g., East Asia,

---

*8   https://www.nier.go.jp/guideline/s31hs/chap5.htm (accessed on December 29, 2017).
*9   https://www.nier.go.jp/guideline/s35h/chap2-2.htm (accessed on December 29, 2017).

West Asia, Europe, etc.) began to be used in the text. Yet it was written in the annotation to the 1970 version that, "it is desirable to create and devise ways to cluster cultural spheres," revealing that the definition of "cultural sphere" had not yet been firmly established."[10] What is obvious from this 1970 version is that the decades-long inclination to explain world history as a dichotomy between the East and the West had become markedly weakened by that time.

In the 1978 version, to describe and understand history through cultural spheres was recommended as if it were the only natural thing to do. Overall, this version of the guideline was permeated with a perception of world history that, while a number of cultural spheres had co-existed and traced their own independent histories during the pre-modern period, unification of the world was promoted by the advancement of modern Europe into various other regions in the world. Nevertheless, only Europe, East Asia, and West Asia alone were explicitly labeled as cultural spheres. Other regions such as South Asia and Southeast Asia were touched on only partly in the explanation of the West Asian cultural sphere.

While both the terms "cultural sphere" and "civilization" were used in the 1989 version, they were treated differently in World History A and World History B. World History A stipulated that students be made to understand the evolution and development of civilizations as well as the cultural characteristics of various regions in the world. World History B, in contrast, described that humankind had adapted to local natural environments and constructed civilizations that later provided the foundation for respective cultural spheres.

The concept of a "regional world" was first used in the 1998 guideline (for both World History A and World History B). The difference between a cultural sphere and a regional world does not become clear just by reading the relevant portion of the guideline. It appears, however, that the concept of regional world was found to be effective in portraying

---

*10 https://www.nier.go.jp/guideline/s45h/chap2-2.htm (accessed on December 29, 2017).

the history of such regions as Southeast Asia, which had been too much under the influence of East Asian and South Asian cultures to be identified as an independent cultural sphere. In the 1998 guideline, frequent references were made to such regional worlds as the Mediterranean world, the inland Asian world, and the Atlantic world. Such references had not been used frequently earlier.

Transition of Views on World History

The perception of world history in postwar Japan has by no means been monolithic. Quite a number of views on world history, including that of the Marxist school, have been proposed and discussed. Yet it is also beyond doubt that high school world history textbooks and the education ministry's curriculum guideline as their endorsing authority have exercised powerful influence on the Japanese people as the standard view of world history. To date, the curriculum guideline's perception of world history has passed through the following three stages:

- **FIRST STAGE (UP TO THE 1960S)**: World history as a combination of the histories of an advanced West (Europe) and a backward East (Asia).

- **SECOND STAGE (FROM 1970 THROUGH THE 1980S)**: In the pre-modern period, multiple cultural spheres emerged to follow separate histories. In the modern period, one of these cultural spheres—the European cultural sphere—took the leadership role in unifying the world.

- **THIRD STAGE (FROM THE 1990S ON)**: Numerous regional worlds in various locations were transformed and reorganized so as to be strongly interconnected. Among these, the European world took the leadership role to unify the world and give it structure.

The transition from the first stage through the third stage reveals that the basic unit for understanding and narrating the history of the world has changed from the dichotomous presence of the East and the West, to multiple cultural spheres and, eventually, to regional worlds. Also, while in earlier stages it had been conceived that a single historical narrative unit corresponding to each specific geographical space existed consistently from past to present, the unit called a "regional world," which was adopted in later stages, was thought of as having been transformed and reorganized.

The Euro-centric understanding and narrative of history—that is, that Europe moves and leads world history—which was clearly seen in early versions of the education ministry's curriculum guidelines, became increasingly inconspicuous, perhaps due to criticisms on it heard from many corners. Thus, the standard view of world history has slowly evolved to date from that of the contrast between a superior Europe (or the West and an inferior Asia (the East) in earlier days to that of the juxtaposition of multiple regional worlds, of which Europe is one.

It should be pointed out, however, that it was a single book, rather than a series of curriculum guidelines, that explicitly proposed for the first time the historical interpretation that the world had evolved from the juxtaposition of multiple cultural spheres into a unified world, which is the standard view of world history in Japan today. Let me introduce this particular book before closing this chapter.

NIHON KOKUMIN NO SEKAISHI

Publication of *Nihon Kokumin no Sekaishi*

More than half a century ago, in 1960, Iwanami Shoten in Tokyo published a book titled *Nihon kokumin no sekaishi* (World history for the Japanese people), co-authored by seven Japanese writers, represented by Uehara Senroku, who greatly influenced research and education on world history in postwar Japan. Originally written as a high school world history textbook, *Nihon kokumin no sekaishi* was rejected by the school textbook screening committee at the education ministry; subsequently, it was published commercially as a book for general readers. It is said that the book was a product of years of discussions among the seven authors, who sometimes got together more than twenty times a year.

Those were the days when the spread of telephones was very limited, not to mention computers or the Internet. In this fruit of their utmost efforts, the seven authors talked fervently about the significance of learning world history. Even today, more than fifty years after the book's publication, those authors' arguments still stir readers' interest. Let us look at the stated purposes of this book.

At the outset of the book's foreword, it is stated, "This *Nihon kokumin no sekaishi* is an attempt at forming an image of world history in response to our need to establish a 'life consciousness' that supports our day-to-day behaviors in the face of the fundamental question of how we, the Japanese people, should live to enjoy a better tomorrow." This "life consciousness" is a rather abstract term, and, admittedly, it is difficult to comprehend. A hint is found in another part of the book, which says, "The life consciousness of today's Japanese people is molded through contemplation on such problems as the construction and maintenance of world peace; the establishment of Japanese independence and autonomy in various political, economic, social, and cultural realms; the improvement of the national standard of living; the elimination of irrationalities from social life; and the securement of individual freedom and dignity."[11] From this, one can conjecture that "life consciousness" means one's consciousness and determination to uphold and realize ideals. Ideals are born because the real world is full of problems. In hope of realizing those ideals, the seven authors of *Nihon kokumin no sekaishi* must have revisited world history in an attempt to clarify why such a problem-stricken world came into being.

This is because, in their words, "The causes of and reasons for the

---

[11] Uehara Senroku, et al. ed., *Nihon kokumin no sekaishi* [World history for the Japanese people] (Tokyo: Iwanami Shoten, 1960), ii.

realities of life of contemporary Japanese people and numerous contributing problems are not to be sought solely inside Japan. Their profound causes are to be found in the footsteps and realities of the Eastern people or the Western people, or both."[12]

The authors go on to claim that it was the aim of the world history that they tried to portray "to take the initiative in exploring how various civilizations in the world have contributed to the development of Japan's civilization and how historical problems that Japan faces today have been affected by movements of these civilizations in the world."[13]

Thus the foreword and a paragraph with the heading "To Learn World History" that appears at the front of the book convey the authors' fervent and sincere determination to look at the realities in Japan squarely and to clarify their root causes so as to consider the future course of Japan.

Concern about Where Japan Stands

It was in 1953, eight years after Japan's defeat in World War II and the year Japan finally regained its independence, that compilation of *Nihon kokumin no sekaishi* was first planned. Thus, it was a matter of course that the greatest concern for the authors was to revise traditional historical understanding from the prewar days and review Japan's past footsteps so as to determine the position of a reborn Japan in the world and the country's future direction. Even though the book's title said the book was about world history, the greatest concern of its authors was undoubtedly Japan itself.

As discussed earlier, a number of historians and historical study groups had continued to explore new directions of historical study since immediately after the defeat in the war. In the early 1950s, a movement called the People's History Movement became active, advocating working and learning together with peasants and workers. The backdrop to this

---

*12 Ibid., ii.
*13 Ibid., ii.

movement was the dynamic world situation of those days: the founding of the People's Republic of China was declared, war erupted on the Korean Peninsula, and the San Francisco Peace Treaty was concluded restoring Japan's sovereignty. It was in the midst of fervent discussions over theory and methods for new historical studies and against the backdrop of this turbulent world situation that *Nihon kokumin no sekaishi* was published.

The arguments put forth by the book's authors were not accepted by the Japanese government, including the Ministry of Education, Science, and Culture. The ministry found the authors' interpretations of contemporary history, including their assessments of the United Nations and socialist countries, as well as their characterization of "peoples of the East" as subjugated and oppressed, to be lopsided. In the end, therefore, the finished manuscript failed to be published as a high school textbook. When instead *Nihon kokumin no sekaishi* was published commercially for general readers, however, it became so widely read that my own copy is from the seventh printing published in 1967, just seven years after the first printing.

The book's seven authors were all well-known historians and intellectuals, and the publisher was a well-known company based in Tokyo. As such, it can be assumed that the view on history advocated by this book must have had a significant impact on Japanese intellectuals and society as a whole in those days. I believe that the outline of the understanding of world history that those seven authors proposed was later adopted by the education ministry's curriculum guideline and passed on until today as the mainstream world history perception in Japan.

Contents of *Nihon Kokumin no Sekaishi*

Let us look at what kinds of histories were contained in *Nihon kokumin no sekaishi*. Excluding the foreword, the explanatory notes, and an introductory essay about learning world history, the book is composed of the following four parts:

PART 1: Origin of Oriental Civilization and Its Advancement
    SECTION 1: Origin of Chinese Civilization and Evolution of East Asian History Surrounding China
    SECTION 2: Origin of Indian Civilization and Its Evolution
    SECTION 3: Origin of West Asian Civilization and Its Evolution

PART 2: Origin of Western Civilization and Its Evolution
PART 3: Modernization of the West and the Rest of the World
PART 4: Contemporary World

Parts 2 through 4 are not subdivided into sections like part 1 is. Rather, they are made of two, six, and four chapters, respectively. Characteristics of the overall description of history in this book can be roughly summarized into the following five points:

1.   This book of world history does not discuss the origin of man or the origin of human civilization in general.

     The authors declare that, "when conducting a historical investigation into the realities of daily life and the real problems in Japan today, perspectives on the eternal strides of humankind ... should be left to human history."[14] It was their position that human history and world history are clearly different, and they were addressing the latter. Therefore, the authors chose to ignore the common past of humankind (or prehistoric days) and wrote the book on the premise that there already had existed a number of mutually different civilizations on earth.

2.   The reality of world history is composed of the Eastern civilization sphere and the Western civilization sphere.

     The authors used civilization as a "collective term to describe all of political, economic, social, and cultural structures and contents with certain historical characteristics that

---

*14 Ibid., 3.

are created through the strides people make."[*15] I must admit that I do not understand how "people" interacted with the broad frameworks of the "East and "West." Nevertheless, it seems beyond doubt that it was the authors' basic understanding that the world is divided between the East and the West, both of which have traced their own distinct histories separately.

3. The Eastern civilization sphere is not a unified entity, and it is subdivided into the East Asian civilization sphere, the Indian civilization sphere, and the West Asian civilization sphere.

    The world is dichotomized as the Western civilization sphere and the Eastern civilization sphere. While the former is perceived to be a unitary entity, the latter is believed to be subdivided into several civilization spheres. The authors were of the view that, prior to modernization in the European civilization sphere, the world was made of a total of four, mutually highly independent civilization spheres—that is, the three spheres within the Eastern civilization sphere plus the European civilization sphere—all of which were simultaneously tracing their own histories. Also, they believed that the history of the Japanese people was molded by trends in the history of the East Asian civilization sphere centered around China. Therefore, the authors claimed that a concrete description of world history for the Japanese people should start with the history of the East Asian civilization sphere. The authors adhered to this in the book.

4. The Western (European) civilization sphere took the leadership role in modernization, and it was in the modern era that a global world order was born around Europe. It was this book's stance that, in contrast to modernized Europe, which actively advanced into various civilization spheres in the Eastern world

---

*15 Ibid., 8–9.

in the realm of politics, economy, and culture, the Eastern civilization sphere reacted passively by accepting such European advancement. In the authors' view, this resulted in the creation of a unified world order around the European peoples by the nineteenth century.

5. The history of the world entered a new phase when World War I ended. "New phase" more concretely refers to the collapse of the Euro-centric world order and the establishment of independence and autonomy for Asian and African peoples as well as expansion of the roles of the United States and the Soviet Union. The authors claimed that, in the contemporary world, four civilization spheres—the Western, the Eastern, the African, and the Soviet—were playing active roles.

Starting Point of Contemporary World History

More than half a century has elapsed since the book's publication, and it seems undeniable that the arguments in *Nihon kokumin no sekaishi* have become somewhat antiquated. Today, the position to discuss world history on the premise of Western superiority in a dichotomized world would be severely criticized as Orientalism, while the notion that the West (Europe) had actively constructed the modern world order would also be censured harshly as a Euro-centric historical view. Also, the Soviet Union, which was supposed to be one of the four components of the contemporary world, has already vanished from the earth.

Nevertheless, in Japan before this book was published, it had been widely believed that the world was divided into the East and the West; they had traced different histories separately; and the West preceded the East. While *Nihon kokumin no sekaishi* basically inherited these notions, it also proposed a new angle on world history based on the view that several civilization spheres had existed simultaneously in the pre-modern era. Even though there were minor modifications in the assessment of the role played by the European civilization sphere, the mainstream argument of the book—that is, that multiple civilization spheres had co-existed before they were gradually integrated to construct a Euro-centric world order—was passed on, basically unchanged, to today's curriculum guideline by the education ministry. It can be said, therefore, that it was this *Nihon kokumin no sekaishi* that created and generalized such a basic understanding of history in Japan.

To be sure, not all of the perceptions of world history held by Uehara and the six other authors were their original ideas. Theirs was a modification of the prewar world history perception based on a dichotomous rivalry between the East and the West in which Japan occupied a delicate position. Also, "civilization sphere" as a unit for understanding and narrating history had already been introduced by Arnold Toynbee in his *A Study of History* published by Oxford University Press in the 1930s. Because an abridged translation of this colossal work by Toynbee was published in Japan in 1949, it can be conjectured that Uehara and his fellow coauthors must have used Toynbee's arguments as a reference. In this sense, the content of *Nihon kokumin no sekaishi* was by no means eccentric. And that was why the world history perspective proposed by this book later became a mainstream understanding of world history in Japan.

CHAPTER 2

PROBLEMS WITH THE PRESENT WORLD HISTORY

DIFFERENT WORLD HISTORIES IN DIFFERENT COUNTRIES

Antiquated Design

The standard perception of world history in Japan today has been slowly molded for more than fifty years. In that sense, it is a sophisticated finished product. It is safe to assume that the overall design of world history that Japanese people carry is more or less fixed. Many historians studying the histories of various regions in the world, such as German history, Russian history, and Islamic world history, accept this overall design, and their research can be likened to adding colors to details or modifying tones here and there.

It is my contention, however, that this design itself has already become antiquated and thus no longer fits the present time. No matter how many layers of colors are painted over the same design, it will still be an antiquated picture. It is time to update the design itself and paint a totally new picture. As of now, the design of this new picture has not yet been determined, and, naturally, no color has been applied yet. This being the case, to conceive a new world history allows historians to use their own originality and ingenuity to decide themes and methods.

There is a step that has to be taken, however, before starting to grope our way forward to drawing a new picture. We must first clarify specifically what in the present world history is out of date and what are the problems. Should we fail to take this step, readers will not fully understand why a new world history is needed. In this chapter, I intend to point out three problems, or limitations, found in the standard view of world history widely accepted in Japan today.

History of One's Own Country and World History

The first problem is that the present standard perception of world history in Japan is a completely Japanese way of perceiving the history of the world. (After all, this is what the title, *Nihon kokumin no sekaishi*, means.) Not all the peoples in the world share the same perception of world history. In today's world, where cross-border human exchanges are widespread, it is not enough for a Japanese to acquire a perception of world history that is valid only in Japan.

As explained in chapter 1, the standard view on world history in Japan is formed on the basis of the curriculum guidelines compiled by the Ministry of Education, Culture, Sports, Science and Technology (MEXT). The education ministry's curriculum guideline attaches much value to the history of Japan and is permeated with the viewpoint of world history as seen from Japan. It should also be noted that, in Japanese high schools, Japanese history is taught as a separate course from world history. For all of these conditions and reasons, in the standard view of world history in Japan, the history of Japan as a nation is built in like an independent cylinder in the overall picture.

That school education is decisive in determining people's historical perception is, to certain extent, also true in other countries besides Japan. Thus, like in Japan, the history taught in schools in various countries attaches much value to that country's own history, and, as a result, history becomes quite different from country to country. One is readily convinced of this if one recalls the heated confrontation of Japan with South Korea and China a few years ago over differences in historical perception. If you participate in international conferences or negotiations, for instance, never doubting that your foreign partner shares the same knowledge about and attitude toward world history, a serious misunderstanding could evolve.

It is often argued that learning world history is meaningful because, by learning other countries' histories, you learn the background of the behaviors and thinking of the people in these countries, which helps you to become friends with them through talking about their history. There is a certain truth in this. In fact, I experienced this personally through the delightful reaction from an Englishman when I talked about the Glorious Revolution of 1689. One time I gave an explanation on Iranian history to an Iranian, who was delighted to find me more knowledgeable about his country's history than himself. Nevertheless, this logic is true only to a certain extent. In actuality, we should be aware that views on world history that are prevalent in Japan are not commonly or universally shared by foreign countries.

While one plus one equals two wherever you are, the content of history classes differs significantly from country to country. To make this point, let me introduce the contents of world history textbooks used in high schools in France (table 3) and China (table 4).

Table 3 lays out the table of contents from a French history textbook. Among the number of interesting observations one can make about this table of contents, let me introduce two here. The first has to do with the spatial range that this textbook covers. As the title of volume two indicates, this history textbook is supposed to address not only French

---

Volume I: Foundation of the Contemporary World, edited by Guillaume Le Quintrec, 2001

Part 1: Examples of Citizenship in Ancient Times
1. Citizens of Athens in 5th Century BCE

Part 2: Birth of Christianity and Its Diffusion
2. Birth of Christianity
3. Diffusion of Christianity

Part 3: The Mediterranean Region in the 12th Century: Crossroads of Three Civilizations
4. Comparison among Christian Occident, Byzantium, and Islam
5. Contacts among Three Civilizations

Part 4: Humanism and Renaissance
6. Humanism and Reformation
7. Renaissance

Part 5: French Revolution and Political Experiences in France up to 1851
8. Last Days of Ancien Régime
9. French Revolution
10. French Consulate and Empire
11. Legacies of the Revolution

Part 6: Europe in the First Half of 19th Century
12. Early Industrial Revolution in Europe
13. Emergence of Industrial Society
14. Liberalism and Nationalism in Europe
15. Europe in 1850

Table 3. Table of Contents of a French History Textbook

Volume II: World, Europe, and France (1850–1945), edited by Jacques Marseille, 2002

Part 1: Era of Industrialization in the Mid-19th Century through 1939

1. Economic Growth and Industrial Society
2. Art, Religion, and Culture in the Era of Industrialization
3. Europe and the Dominated World

Part 2: France between the Mid-19th Century and 1914

4. Impediments and Vitality of France (1848–1914)

5. From One Republic to Another (1848–79)
6. Firmly Embedded Republic (1880–1914)

Part 3: War, Democracy, and Totalitarianism

7. World War I
8. Crisis of Liberal Democracy—France in the 1930s
9. Totalitarian Regime
10. Aspects of World War II
11. Nazi's Massacre Policy
12. France during World War II

Volume III: World, Europe, and France after 1945 to the Present, edited by Guillaume Le Quintrec, 2004

Part 1: World after 1945 to the Present

1. World in 1945
2. From Industrial Society to Telecommunication and Information Society
3. Two Models of Regime Ideology
4. East-West Confrontation until the 1970s
5. Ex-Colony Third World toward the end of the 1970s
6. Quest for New World Order since the 1970s
7. Middle East after 1945 to the Present

Part 2: Europe after 1945 to the Present

8. Construction of Western Europe from 1945 to 1989
9. Era of People's Democracy
10. Europe's Challenges after 1989

Part 3: France after 1945 to the Present

11. Outcome of World War II and Memories
12. Political Conditions after 1945 to the Present
13. Economy, Society, and Culture after 1945 to the Present
14. France in the World after 1945

SOURCE: Guillaume Le Quintrec, *Histoire 2de: livre de l'élève* (Paris: Nathan, 2001). Jacques Marseille, *Marseille: Histoire, 1ère, Bac L, ES* (Paris: Nathan, 2003). Guillaume Le Quintrec, *Histoire, terminale L-ES* (Paris: Nathan, 2004).

history but also the history of the entire world. In the Japanese context, it is like the history of Japan and the history of the world combined. Nevertheless, throughout all three volumes, coverage is limited mostly to the history of France and its peripheral areas. More concretely, many references are made to Greece and Byzantium in ancient times and to European countries from the nineteenth century on.

A quick glance at this table of contents reveals that in this textbook Japan is mentioned first in the description of the Russo-Japanese War, in which only a single line is spent on the Meiji Restoration. After that, an illustration of territories occupied by the Japanese military in the section on World War II is just about the only conspicuous reference to Japan. There is no reference to Japan before the Meiji Restoration—that is, Japan during the Edo period (1603–1868). This is a stark contrast to Japan's world history textbooks, which devote much space to not only the French Revolution but also French history since ancient times. As far as this textbook can tell, it seems safe enough to assume that the average French person knows next to nothing about Japan's past unless he/she has special interest in this country.

And this is not a phenomenon unique to France alone. Space does not allow me to go into details, but as far as I know, the situation is quite similar in Britain and the Netherlands, too. In European schools, it is customary to pay little attention to non-European countries, including those in Asia, unless the reference is tied to something directly related to their own histories. (Thus, histories of former colonies such as India and Indonesia are important topics in the history classes of Britain and the Netherlands, respectively.)

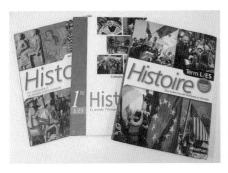

Figure 2. High School History Textbooks in France (Photo taken by the author)

The second interesting observation one can make from the table of contents is that this textbook employs the format of picking up a few key topics and adding commentaries to them, instead of laying out and describing historical events chronologically. This format is typical in volume one on the pre-mid-nineteenth century. Thus, for instance, Byzantine and Islamic civilizations make abrupt appearances as something that had already existed all along. The textbook does not adopt the method of describing the evolution of these civilizations chronologically from their genesis, like Japanese textbooks do.

In the other two volumes, too, historical events are not always narrated or described according to chronological sequences and, instead, characteristics of selected political and social incidents in each period are often introduced in a conceptual model. In other words, the method of explanation based on "A causes B" or "A is transformed to B" is not considered to be absolute. And this is where French textbooks differ widely from Japanese history textbooks, which rely on diachronic history unquestionably. This point will be revisited in chapter 4.

In any event, the content of this textbook is subtly different from French history as we know it in Japan. It is, of course, different from European history (or the history of the West), too. That being the case, it must be quite difficult for a Japanese person, who has learned world history in a Japanese high school, and a French person, who was taught history in a French high school, to share knowledge on world history and the histories of each other's countries. On that basis, then, it must also be difficult for them to conduct business talks or discussions in international conferences.

World History Textbook of China

History education in China today is comprised of the history of China and the history of the world. The composition of history with two pillars is a feature that China's history education shares with Japan, unlike history education in France. But, of course, the contents of Chinese textbooks differ greatly from their Japanese counterparts. In China, the history of Japan is part of world history, while Chinese history is taught separately. Let us look into the content of Chinese textbooks first.

In China, high schools across the country do not use the same textbook, and the textbooks used differ from region to region. Among those textbooks, let

Figure 3. High School World History Textbooks in China (Photo taken by the author)

me introduce in table 4 the table of contents of the second edition of *Shijie tongshi* (Overview of world history) edited by Wang Side. Like the French textbook, this textbook also consists of three volumes.

This Chinese textbook differs significantly from the French one in its universal coverage of the histories of various regions in the world and explanations of incidents in accordance with the chronological sequence of their occurrence. In this sense, the Chinese textbook is more akin to its Japanese counterparts. Nevertheless, there also are a number of differences between the two. For instance, the Chinese textbook adopts such periodizations as "pre-industrialization civilization," "feudal civilization," and "industrial civilization"—concepts rarely heard of in Japan. Also, terms such as "capitalism" and "socialism" are referred to much more often than in Japanese textbooks, which, after all, might only be expected in a textbook from a socialist country. Aside from these points, Japanese eyes will readily spot such peculiarities as the absence of reference to the Islamic world and the place that Japan is given in world history, which is quite different from what is taught in Japan. (For example, Japan is regarded as one of the major powers of the world in prewar days, and it is also defined as a fascist state.)

But the most striking difference by far is the dearth of reference to the history of China in world history. While Japanese students are taught about the Yellow River civilization as one of the ancient civilizations, world history taught in Chinese high schools does not include it. The

Table 4. Table of Contents of a Chinese Textbook of World History

3. New Faces of Contemporary
   Society
4. Innovation in Scientific Civilization and Advancement

**Chapter 8: World Powers in the
Wave of the Second
Industrial Revolution**

1. Britain Challenged
2. Advancing France

3. Rising Germany
4. Rapidly Developing United
   States
5. Russia Where Tradition and
   Modernity Interact
6. Expanding Japan

**Volume III: Development of Contemporary Civilization and Options—
World History in the 20th Century**

**Chapter 1: Trends and Structure of
the World in the Early
20th Century**

1. World under Domination by
   Great Powers
2. Local Clashes during World
   Structural Transition
3. World War I
4. Versailles Treaty–Nine Power
   Treaty System

**Chapter 2: Socialist Soviet Union's
Pursuit of Modernization
Drive**

1. Eruption of the Russian Revolution
2. October Revolution of 1917
   and Construction of the Soviet
   Regime
3. Soviet Russian Exploration of
   the Socialist Line
4. Establishment of the Stalin Style

**Chapter 3: Trends and Adjustments
in Capitalist Regimes**

1. Prosperity of the Capitalist
   World and Peace in the 1920s
2. Reformism Movement and

Social Democrats' Participation
in Government
3. Rise of World Fascist Movement
4. 1929–33 Major Crisis of the
   Capitalist World Economy and
   Self-Adjustment by the Capitalist Regime

Chapter 4: World War II

1. Abrogation of Treaties by Fascist
   States and Military Expansion
2. The Collective Security System
   and Conciliatory Policy
3. From Local War to All-out War
4. Shift of War Strategy and
   Victory of Anti-Fascist Coalition
5. From Teheran to Potsdam—
   Setup of Postwar World by War
   Winners

**Chapter 5: Beginning of the East-
West Cold War**

1. Reorganization of the Capitalist
   System
2. Formation of the Socialist Camp
3. U.S.-USSR Cold War
4. Important Clashes in Early
   Years of the Cold War

Chapter 6: Science and Technology Revolution and Development of Postwar Capitalism

1. Postwar Science and Technology Revolution and Its Impact
2. State Monopolistic Capitalism in the United States and Its Development
3. Restoration and Unification of Western Europe
4. Rapid Growth of Japan's Economy
5. Economic Crisis in the 1970s and Readjustment of Capitalism
6. Socialist Movements in Capitalist Countries Developed after WWII

Chapter 7: Development and Transformation of Postwar Soviet Union and East European Countries

1. Footsteps of Postwar Soviet Union
2. Transformation of East European Countries
3. Drastic Transformation of East Europe and Dissolution of the Soviet Union

Chapter 8: People's Liberation Movements in the 20th Century and Modernization Policy of Developing Countries

1. Rise of People's Liberation Movements
2. Postwar Surge of Independence Movements and Collapse of Colonial Rules
3. Modernization Policy of Developing Countries

Chapter 9: Multipolarization of the World

1. Division of the World into Two Camps
2. Rise of the Third World
3. U.S.-Soviet Quest for Hegemony
4. End of Two-Camp Era

Chapter 10: Development of 20th-Century Thought and Culture

1. Philosophy and Historical Studies
2. Literature and Art
3. Religion

SOURCE: Source: Wang Side, ed. *Shijie tongshi* [Overview of world history], 2nd edition (Shanghai: East China Normal University Press, 2009).

histories of pre-revolution dynasties, such as Tang, Song, or Qing, are nowhere to be seen. Moreover, the founding of the People's Republic of China or China's behavior during the cold war are not even referred to, not to mention the Xinhua Revolution. From the textbook, it looks as if China had had no influence on the world, and as if world history were complete without China. Chapter 6 of volume 2 on the "Clash of

Two Civilizations in Asia" mainly addresses the British colonization of India. The absence of reference in this chapter to Britain's military and economic advancement into China beginning with the Opium Wars feels strange to the Japanese. The mysterious absence of these important elements from world history in China seems to be attributable to the inclination to regard everything that has anything to do with China as Chinese incidents to be addressed in textbooks of Chinese history instead.

The most recent world history curriculum guidelines compiled by the MEXT repeatedly stresses the importance of paying close attention to the positioning of Japan in world history. The Chinese textbook, on the other hand, does not seem to stress such a special consideration. On the contrary, world history and the history of China are clearly separated to form two perfectly independent pillars. It should not be easy for the Chinese who learn history based on this textbook and the Japanese who are taught world history through Japanese textbooks to share common understandings on world history.

Different World Histories in Different Countries

Just a glance at history textbooks used in France and China makes us easily imagine that people in different countries around the world must have different perceptions of world history. There is a Chinese version of world history in China and a Japanese version in Japan. World history is perceived in France as something totally different from how it is perceived in Japan and China. When people belonging to different countries talk about world history, they find that their respective perceptions of history, on which they base their arguments, are subtly different from each other.

This might have been fine if we were living in the late nineteenth to early twentieth century. During this period, when the concept and structure of the nation-state, such as France and Japan, were in the making, people in each country were expected to be aware that they belonged to their states as, say, French and Japanese nationals. In that sense, it was important for each country to have its own national history. It was taken for granted that other countries had their own national histories and, in fact, world history hardly became the subject for arguments. Probably people only vaguely considered that the combination of their own history and the histories of other countries would make up world history. The situation is totally different today, when it is a serious problem that people in the world do not share a common world history. The time has come for us to seriously discuss world history.

WORLD HISTORY TO ENDORSE REALITY

History to Demarcate Oneself from Others

The second problem of the standard view on world history in Japan is its inclination to emphasize the differences between one group of individuals and other groups. The basic view on the world and its history that high school students and ordinary people in Japan acquire by studying the subject in high school can be summarized as follows.

There are a great number of countries in the world aside from Japan, and each one of them has its own history. If all of these histories of different countries are put together, you have world history. The East Asian civilization (or regional world) also has its own history, which is different from the history of European civilization, including Britain, France, and Germany, located in western Eurasia.

Once this view is taken in, it is imprinted in one's mind, almost unconsciously, that we the Japanese and peoples of other countries/ regions have different histories and, therefore, we do not belong to a same community. To put it differently, world history as we know it is envisioned and described on the basis of the perception of the world as a mixed bag of different civilizations and countries. It can be labeled a world history that presupposes differences between oneself and others.

Seeing as the actual world is made up of numerous sovereign states, it can be said that this world history endorses the reality of the world. Some may find nothing wrong with that. But, let us pause here and look back at the path we have travelled. Modern historical studies, which advocated primary source–based empiricism since its establishment in the nineteenth century, exercised great influence on the birth of the nation-state—a totally new development for human society—by "creating" histories of each country and its people. When a country and its people have their own history, they are recognized as a real presence. Thus, the empirical study of the history of a country and its people, which used the academic method to pursue truth, became a powerful support in the construction of a nation-state. In a somewhat different way, Marxist historical studies constructed a general theory on the developmental stages of humankind, which, at one time, played a major political and cultural role as a guideline for the future.

As I have explained, historical studies and its products in the past played an important role in pointing human society in the direction it should take, for better or worse. Present-day world history and historical studies, which only endorse the present reality, however, do not have such political, social, or cultural power. Unlike historical studies in the past, which was a guiding light of the times, today's historical studies seem to be watching the course of history from behind, in blank surprise. It seems to be high time for those in the historical research profession to once again seriously contemplate the social significance of historical studies.

This aspiration of historians aside, historical studies has hitherto been good at portraying the history of each human group and accentuating their different characteristics, be it such nation-state history as the history of Japan or such history of civilizations or regional worlds as European history. Take these statements, for example: "Japanese society in the seventeenth to eighteenth centuries was characterized by a unique form of government called *bakuhan* system (the shogunate and domain system of administration)," "The European and Islamic worlds have two different histories," and "Secularization of society is a unique feature of European history." Through these characterizations, people have obtained their sense of belonging to, say, Japan or Europe. And it has been understood that all of these different histories bound together comprise world history. World history as we know it, then, is an aggregate of separate and mutually unrelated "regional" histories.

This mental tendency to understand the world in a clear dichotomy between oneself and others is still at work, more or less, everywhere in the world. And it is the self-consciousness of northwestern European intellectuals of the nineteenth century that has so strongly influenced today's people. Their dichotomic self-consciousness (i.e., oneself vs. others) was a powerful tool that elevated nationalistic sentiment and provided a centripetal force for those groups of individuals that accepted it. Yet, at the same time, such thinking often led to conflicts between "we" and "they." This worldview in which one demarcates oneself from others is actually one of the causes of the numerous conflicts and battles that have been repeated everywhere in the world since the nineteenth century.

Thus, modern historical studies, which was completed by northwestern European intellectuals in the nineteenth century, has naturally both encompassed this dichotomic worldview as a framework of historical research and endorsed it.

Substantiation of the Islamic World

Let us take up one concrete example here to point out the problems of the world history based on the dichotomic division between oneself and others. The example is Islamic world history.

The following conversation took place quite some time ago, when I was writing the book *Isuramu sekai no sōzō* (Creating the notion of the Islamic world), which was published in 2005 by the University of Tokyo Press. In the course of a casual talk at the university with one of my colleagues from the science department, he asked me about the specific theme of my research. When I said, "I am contemplating what the Islamic world is all about and whether such a thing really exists," my colleague retorted, "But there is an Islamic world, isn't there? I learned about it in my high school world history class." At this point, it occurred to me, all of a sudden, that that was what the learning of history does to you. Today, I am deeply grateful to this colleague for inadvertently giving me an important hint.

Whatever the object is, whether it is a person, a group of people, goods, or space, if one can write the history of that object, it automatically means that the object exists or existed in the past. You cannot write the history of something that did not/does not exist. Many Japanese believe in the existence of the Islamic world because they learn the history of the Islamic world in their high school history class. In other words, world history contributes to the substantiation of the Islamic world in people's minds.

Needless to say, world history alone does not substantiate the concept of the Islamic world. Intellectuals, politicians, bureaucrats, and the mass media of Japan and the rest of the world are to blame even more. They blindly believe in the dichotomic worldview of the West vs. the Islamic world and consolidate and reproduce comments based on this worldview.

Let's look at an example. On Constitution Memorial Day on May 3, 2007, the daily *Asahi Shimbun* carried twenty-one editorials under the title, "21 Editorials: Proposals on Japan's New Strategy." One of those twenty-one editorials was entitled, "How to get along with Islam." As the title suggests, this editorial discussed how to get along with the Islamic world—"one of the 'others'" for Japan. Allow me to quote a few sentences that represent the position of this editorial well.

For instance, the editorial said, "How should Japan get along with Islam? Japan should be able to construct a more receptive strategy toward it by utilizing its own history as a country that has developed under non-Western culture," "The Islamic world tends to aspire to a development model of its own that is different from so-called westernization," "It might be an idea to set up a national research center of Islamic studies in Japan … to increase contact points with the Islamic world," and "It will be an investment in the future for Japan to actively nurture human resources who can make contacts with the Islamic world."

Common to the above statements is the emphasis that the Islamic world is a unique space that is different from the West or from Japan. Seeing as I have written on this issue in detail elsewhere,[*16] I will refrain from repeating myself here. Let me point out, instead, that the Islamic world discussed by the editorial was not only a space with a certain, albeit ambiguous, geographical range, but also a virtual space for seeing all Muslims as one unit. The argument in the editorial was structured on the premises that such a space does exist on earth and that it is different from Japan, a space that we belong to. This was an argument based on the worldview and method for discussing history that has developed in Japan for more than 100 years. This editorial recognized the Islamic world as having a real existence, and that should have been easy for the majority of the readers to accept.

But I am urged to argue that, as long as we, the Japanese people, regard the Islamic world and Muslims as "others," who are different from us and, on that basis, discuss how to get along with them, fundamental problems will never be solved. What is called for is for us to take on problems in such places as Iraq, Afghanistan, and Palestine as our own, instead of considering them "their" problems, and to tackle those problems together with people in the troubled areas. While a demarcation between oneself and others is inevitable, we need to envision a higher, larger self that extends over and above the "us and them" dichotomy.

The new world history that I am proposing surely has the power to create this higher and larger self. We should not continue to stick to the kind of history that could, by stressing differences between ourselves and others, produce seeds of conflict. It is high time for us to change our way of thinking. What is called for today is both an understanding of history that pays more attention to commonalities rather than differences and a portrayal of world history based on this understanding.

---

*16 Haneda Masashi, "Isuramu sekai to atarashii sekaishi" [The Islamic world and new world history], *Gurōbaru hisutorī no chōsen* [Challenge of global history], Mizushima Tsukasa, ed. (Tokyo: Yamakawa Shuppansha, 2008).

China and the Islamic World

At the risk of digressing somewhat from the subject of this book, I'd like to discuss here how insensitive and unqualified the use of the concept of the Islamic world has been in Japan. In the earlier discussion of world history taught in China today, I pointed out that the term "Islamic world" is not used in China. Chinese textbooks use the term "Arabic civilization," instead of the "Islamic world" or the "Islamic civilization" that are referred to in Japan. Because China has a large Muslim population, the term "Islamic world" is, at least officially, something of a taboo. If the Islamic world were viewed as a real space, it would partially overlap with the Chinese territory, which could challenge the integrity of China as a unity.

Unlike Japan, where nobody doubts the real existence of the Islamic world, the concept is, therefore, a highly sensitive one in China. In his inauguration speech in January 2009, President Barack Obama proposed reconciliation with Muslims in the world and said, "To the Muslim world, we seek a new way forward, based on mutual interest and mutual respect." The Xinhua News Agency, the official press agency of the People's Republic of China, posted a translation of the full text of this speech on its website, but it is reported that this sentence related to the Islamic world was entirely deleted.[*17]

If China's large Muslim population started identifying themselves more strongly as believers of Islam than as Chinese nationals, it would be highly troublesome for the Chinese government. Muslims residing in China, such as the Uyghurs, who have been in a highly unstable position as a minority, are liable to collude with Muslims abroad to start a movement that could shake up the entire state system of China. For the Chinese government, the Islamic world is an extremely dangerous spatial concept that cannot be shrugged off as something of "their" world.

Although President Obama had referred to the "Muslim world" in his inauguration speech, he later stopped using this term. This might be because the "Muslim world" used in the singular could project an

---

[*17] *Asahi Shimbun* (morning edition, January 28, 2009).

image that it is a homogenous space equipped with its own will like a nation-state. In his June 4, 2009, speech in Cairo, Egypt, therefore, President Obama cautiously used such plural forms as "Muslims around the world" and "Muslim-majority countries." It appeared that the Obama administration had decided to face reality squarely and take a courteous attitude toward Muslims.

Nevertheless, the Japanese media covering this speech still used the term "Islamic world" when they reported that while in Cairo the U.S. president had proposed collaboration with the Islamic world. Compared to President Obama's sensitivity to cautiously change his expression in order to promote reconciliation, whether it was effective or not, it must be said that the Japanese media were almost in a state of brain freeze as far as reference to the Islamic world was concerned. I am of the view that the Japanese media have been insensitive to (1) the risk that such a vague term as the "Islamic world" could be misunderstood; (2) the tendency for this term to be politically charged; and (3) the danger that use of this term makes people miss some important points. Japan, which, unlike China, has almost no Muslim population, can afford to use this term to conveniently describe a space that is inhabited by people who are different from its own.

EURO-CENTRIC HISTORICAL VIEW

The Most Serious Fault of the Present World History

The third problem with the world history that is prevalent in today's Japan is its Euro-centric historical view. Closely related to the first and second problems already discussed, this third problem is, in my opinion, the most serious fault to be found in the present-day perception of world history. I say this because, if the Japanese people learn world history as it is taught in school, they are almost automatically made to believe that Europe is the most superior, special presence in the world.

Incidentally, in Japan, "Europe" is often used as a synonym for Europe plus the United States. But this is a kind of fantasy, because Europe and the United States are different from one another in a number of features. Nonetheless, in this book Europe is used in the subsequent discussion of the Euro-centric historical view as a synonym for Europe plus the United States, which is almost equivalent to the West.

Simply put, the Euro-centric historical view is summarized as follows:

Europe makes history; the rest of the world has none until it is brought into contact with Europe. Europe is the center; the rest of the world is its periphery. Europeans alone are capable of initiating change or modernization; the rest of the world is not.[*18]

The European history that was portrayed by the people in the nineteenth century who believed that they belonged to Europe was there to distinguish Europe from other areas as something special and to clarify the origin of its superiority. The outline of that history is as follows: Europe rediscovered the wisdom of ancient civilizations during the Renaissance era; deprived churches of traditional powers through the Reformation; developed science and technology and reformed political and economic systems in places into which Europeans advanced during the Age of Exploration; underwent the American War of Independence, the French Revolution, and Britain's Industrial Revolution; and eventually became a world hegemon in the nineteenth century. This is a success story, and, if you will, the history of a winner.

The above outline still remains very much intact in the Japanese understanding of world history today. Let us take a look at, for example, the structure of *Shōsetsu sekaishi B* (Detailed account of world history B), the textbook published by Tokyo's Yamakawa Shuppansha and used by the largest number of high schools. In this textbook, the histories

---

*18 Robert B. Marks, *The Origins of the Modern World* (2nd edition) (Lanham: Rowman & Littlefield, 2007), 8.

of the sixteenth through nineteenth centuries are clustered together in Part III, which consists of the following seven chapters:

CHAPTER 8: Prosperity of Various Regions in Asia
CHAPTER 9: Birth of Modern Europe
CHAPTER 10: Development of the Sovereign State System in Europe
CHAPTER 11: Growth of Modern Societies in Europe and North America
CHAPTER 12: Development of the Modern Nation-State in Europe and North America
CHAPTER 13: Turmoil in Asian Countries
CHAPTER 14: Imperialism and Nationalist Movements in Asia

Four chapters from chapter 9 through chapter 12 are devoted to the birth of modern Europe and its evolution in chronological sequence. In contrast, the history of various regions in Asia is explained in separate chapters: the prosperity in Asia in the sixteenth through seventeenth centuries is discussed in chapter 8, while chapter 13 discusses the turmoil in Asia in the eighteenth to nineteenth centuries and chapter 14 explains how many Asian regions became colonized and how nationalist movements were organized there to resist Europe's imperialistic rule.

Undoubtedly, those who learn world history from this textbook are inevitably imprinted with the following understanding of history: while Europe may have been on a par with other regional worlds earlier, it advanced ahead of others in economic development after the sixteenth century, to which non-European regional worlds had to subjugate themselves; Europe was also ahead of others in creating new political mechanisms, ideas, and values, encounters with which shook up backward non-European regions, forcing them to accept these European inventions, willingly or unwillingly.

In this view, only Europe advanced and succeeded. As long as this European history (which in Japan is often synonymous to the history of the West) is incorporated in world history in a way that distinguishes it from the history of other regions, and as long as we accept this view uncritically, the stance that interprets world history around Europe and the worldview that Europe is the center of the world and superior to others will never change.

To be sure, the economic power and military might of some of the northwestern European countries had been outstandingly superior to other countries (including many which are geographically categorized as European countries) in the period up to the late nineteenth century. In today's world, when it is obvious to anyone that the will of European countries is not the sole mover of the life of people throughout the world, however, this kind of historical view that demarcates Europe from non-Europe and stresses its unparalleled superiority should no longer be supported.

It should be noted that an inclination to understand the past by placing themselves in the center of events is more or less seen in any group of people in the world and, therefore, is not a characteristic unique to Europe alone. In fact, as we will see in the next chapter, similar examples are found almost limitlessly, including the Sino-centric view of history, the Islam-centric view of history, and the Japan-centric view of history. In this sense, the act of those who feel a sense of belonging to Europe to portray a Euro-centric history itself should not be criticized. The problem is that even those who are segregated from Europe as non-European, including the Japanese, readily accept the concept of Europe and the understanding of world history centered around Europe.

Survival of European History

Efforts to overcome this Euro-centric historical view have been pursued continuously here and there in the world. People residing in Europe themselves often admit that the history of Europe is not special and should not be treated as something special. In Japan, also, in compliance with MEXT's curriculum guideline, the view that world history is a conglomerate of the histories of numerous cultural spheres or regional worlds in which European history is just one has been established to a considerable extent. It appears that, as tenacious as the Euro-centric historical view might have been, it is finally on the verge of being side-lined in Japan.

But is this really so? I, for one, suspect that things are not that simple. It seems true that the Euro-centric historical view has been rel-ativized. And yet, I do not think that we can declare that the perception of the world and the view of world history that are prevalent in today's Japan are totally divorced from the Euro-centric historical view. In fact, such comments as "Japan is behind the West by x number of years," "Japan should follow the West and catch up with it," and "the West advanced while Japan closed its door to foreign countries" are still ram-pant in Japan. When exhibitions of the Hapsburgs or of Impressionist painting are held, they are without fail swarmed by visitors. Department stores frequently sponsor such events as a "France festival" or an "Ital-ian fair." In Japan, the British Museum is called *Daiei Hakubutsukan* ("Great" British Museum), and nobody questions the anachronistic tone of the translation. Even though in the Edo period Nagasaki was mostly a port for trade with China, it is repeatedly emphasized as a "gateway to European civilization." Local municipalities in Kyushu where Dutch or Portuguese ships had visited in the past are eager to conclude sister city agreements with Dutch and Portuguese counterparts in order to honor those contacts of the past. These are just a few examples of statements and behaviors derived from the Euro-centric historical view that are still rampant around us.

A more focused analysis of the most recent curriculum guideline will provide us with the reason for the above phenomena. MEXT's curriculum guideline compiled in 2009 states that there existed multiple cultural spheres or regional worlds around the world. Nevertheless, all the cul-tural spheres or regional worlds outside Europe were found in either the New World or what used to be called the Orient. While non-Europe, which used to be treated as a unitary presence, was disintegrated into several regional worlds, the framework and description of European history has been largely untouched and essentially retains the features of the history of the Western world as it was taught in prewar days, separated from other regions in the world. While Europe has become one of cultural spheres, it still holds its special position. The diachronic description of its history has been preserved without experiencing major changes.

Mystery of European History

The term "Europe," which is used in Japan when discussing world history, usually refers to a regional world on a par with such other regional worlds as East Asia and South Asia. And it is considered that a distinct history has evolved in Europe within a framework of geographical space segregated from other spaces. There is a view that an important significance of the Islamic culture lies in its role to preserve classical ancient cultures within itself before transmitting them to Europe. This typically Euro-centric historical interpretation is possible only when Europe is viewed as an independent geographical space.

The description of European history that is prevalent today, however, does not necessarily correspond to the past of Europe as a geographical space. This becomes apparent when we give thought to the degree of consistency between the pasts of East Europe, Scandinavia, and South Europe and the narrative that we normally think of as European history.

Let us take an example of Spain and Portugal. It is usually explained that, in the fifteenth to sixteenth centuries, these two countries were the central figures in the "expansion of Europe," chasing off Muslims from the Iberian Peninsula and advancing into various non-European regions themselves. When nineteenth-century Europe is discussed, however, these two countries are hardly referenced. This is because it is countries like Britain, France, and Germany that represent Europe in this period. To understand the reason, one need only ask whether industrial revolution, free trade, and democracy—that is, the three key indices that demarcate nineteenth-century Europe from non-Europe—were seen in Spain and Portugal in this period. The answer to this question is, of course, no. As a matter of fact, it was probably only in the fifteenth to sixteenth centuries that the pasts of these two countries fit well within the main story of European history. It is hard to imagine that the overview of the histories of these two countries would naturally fit with that of European history. Perhaps a similar thing can be said about Norway, which is referred to only during the Viking Age, and Italy, which is not talked about until the nineteenth-century founding of the nation-state after the Renaissance.

When it comes to that, actually, there are other mysterious things about European history. Not the least among them is the chronological division applied only to the history of western Eurasia and the Mediterranean region during a specific period, which is not seen in the case of eastern and southern Eurasia. This region's history is divided into two between the earlier period in which it was made of the Ancient Orient and the Mediterranean world and the later period in which the same region was composed of the Islamic world and Europe. When such regions as the East Asian world and the South Asian world are believed to have consistently existed from of old as a geographical space, why is the European world different? Isn't Europe a geographical space? It is hard to accept the Islamic world as a geographical space because it is envisioned around the nucleus of a religion. And if these two were not geographical spaces, what is this "regional world" that we accept today in world history all about? I must say that its criteria are very ambiguous. Shelving this issue momentarily, Europe as a geographical name does exist on a map. Why the history of this geographical space called Europe is not portrayed with consistency from the past all the way to the present is a mystery.

Two Europes

At this point, let us sort out my argument so far. The key point is that the term "Europe" is both a geographical space and an abstract concept as well. The etymological origin of the term dates back to Ancient Greece. For instance, Herodotus, a Greek historian of the fifth century BCE, considered that the world was composed of Europe, Asia, and Libya (Africa). The line connecting the Bosphorus in the south and the Tanais (Don) river, which poured into the Black Sea, in the north was the boundary between Europe and Asia. In the west Eurasian Catholic world until the fourteenth to fifteenth centuries, the term "Europe" was used to identify the land that they lived in, and, therefore, it basically referred to a geographical space. Because it was their habitat, it would not be surprising if people living there were inclined to add some positive or constructive images to the term. The T and O Map (fig. 4), which represented the worldview in this period, shows, however, that Europe was just one part of a world divided into three. The center of the world for Christians in those days was Jerusalem.

Yet it was not until the early to mid-nineteenth century that

Figure 4. T and O Map

The T and O map represents the physical world as first described by the seventh-century scholar Isidore of Seville in his *Etymologiae*. Asia occupies the top half, while Europe in the lower left was only a quarter of the world.

SOURCE: The first printed edition of *Etymologiae, XIV: de terra et partibus*, representing the inhabited world. Augsburg, 1472.

the substance of Europe as a concept became consolidated. All the values that were thought to be positive in those days were connected with attributes of Europe by intellectuals of northwestern Europe and North America. Such attributes as progress, democracy, freedom, equality, science, secular, and universal were among the values. This contributed to making the substance of Europe as a concept quite complex and unique. It should be noted, though, that this complex and unique concept does not necessarily represent characteristics of the society of people who dwelled in the geographical space called Europe. These are just attributes of Europe as a concept. Europe projects positive images more explicitly when it is compared with such contrasting concepts as the Orient (which is opposite to the Occident), Asia, and the Islamic world. Henceforth in this book, Europe will be set in quotation marks, i.e. "Europe," when it explicitly refers to Europe as a concept.

The fundamental problem of the European history that we learn in school is that the history belonging to "Europe" as a concept, on the one hand, and the past of Europe as a geographical space, on the other, are not explicitly demarcated. Rather, together they form a complete whole. As I have repeatedly pointed out, conventional European history is a product of the self-consciousness and worldview of those people in the nineteenth century who believed that they were a special existence. The "Europe" that these people believed in and many others accepted is a concept, and it does not coincide with the real life geographical space. The world history that embraces the history of "Europe" as a concept can never be free from the Euro-centric historical view. As I have explained in the discussion of the second problem of the standard view on world history in Japan, the history of "Europe" is bound to distinguish itself from others and stresses its superiority.

European History of the Japanese People

A tone of caution is in order before closing this chapter. The European history that is taught in Japan is not always 100 percent equal to the European history that is understood by those who regard themselves as "European." Even when the concept of "Europe" became powerful in the nineteenth century, there were not too many occasions for an integrated European history to be studied and portrayed in European countries. It was because in those days the consolidation of their individual national histories was prioritized in each of the European countries. For instance, Jules Michelet, a renowned French historian in the nineteenth century, stressed the importance and superiority of French history, declaring, "There is always something amiss in the histories of other countries. It is only the French history that is perfect" in his *Le Peuple* (1846).[*19]

Even today, it appears that a combination of the history of one's own country and that of neighboring countries which have had relations with it is vaguely understood as European history in many of the countries

---

*19 Jules Michelet, *Le peuple,* 5e édition (Paris: Calmann-Lévy, 1877), 275.

in the region. While they all share a broad framework from which the history of the non-European region is excluded, there is nevertheless no common European history that is accepted in all of the European countries. Each country has its own European history. Now that the European Union (EU) has come to take on a significant meaning as a political and economic unity, historians in concerned countries have finally begun to make an attempt at portraying an integrated European history.

In contrast, European history, or the history of the West, has been constantly at the center of the study of histories of foreign countries in Japan since the Meiji era, except for a brief period during World War II. Even though this European history is, in actuality, an aggregation of the histories of individual European countries including British history, German history, and French history, there has been a strong tendency in Japan to understand the histories of the Western world countries by integrating them in a framework of history of the Western world. In that sense, it may be said that the Japanese view of world history is closer to the historical view of the United States, where people tend to unify Europe and North America into the West and understand its history in that framework. In the case of Japan, the Western world carries the strong implication of an idealized advanced region that Japan should emulate. In this sense, the concept and framework of the history of the Western world became a breeding ground for uniquely Japanese Occidentalism.

In today's Japan, we still say "In Europe, …" often to support our arguments. But, as becomes obvious once one actually visits European countries, "Europe" is not such an obvious and unified presence. Allow me to introduce my personal experience. I still cannot overcome the astonishment and the gap I sensed when I flew to Italy in the winter of 1997 from Britain, where I had spent close to ten months. Of course, the color and shape of buildings were different, and so were the vegetation and meals, but those differences were not the only causes of my reaction. Britain was a cloudy northern country where order-loving, calm, reserved, but stubborn people lived, while people in Italy living in chaotic towns under the bluest sky were cheerful and hot-tempered, but extremely flexible. What a stark contrast! I did not find it possible to put them together and call all of them Europeans. Then I wondered if we in Japan had formed a unique image of Europe as an idealized and unified "Europe" thanks to the great geographical distance.

Needless to say, British people in the nineteenth century never defined themselves as Europeans. For the majority of British people, Europe was a different world over there across the Strait of Dover. If that is indeed the case, the Euro-centric historical view prevalent in Japan, which I have repeatedly underscored in this book, might be slightly different from the Euro-centric historical view shared by European countries themselves, and it might be charged with uniquely Japanese characteristics. Space does not allow me to go further into this issue here, but it is definitely worth examining some other time.

Thus, so far, I have tried to explain why the present world history is out of step with our times and, therefore, problematic from the following three angles:

1. The world history prevalent in Japan today is the world history for the Japanese people;

2. Present-day world history emphasizes demarcation between oneself and others; and

3. The world history of today is not free from the Euro-centric historical view.

These three problems of present-day world history in Japan, actually, share a root. That root is modern historical studies itself, which was firmly established in the nineteenth century, because this historical studies harbors these three problems. It demarcates Europe (oneself) from non-Europe (others) and envisions a world history that is made of "our own history" and the history of other countries, which are two different things.

If this is indeed the case, do we really have no other choice than to discard the method and outcomes of modern historical studies altogether and to come up with a totally new method of perceiving the past of humankind? I am not that pessimistic. I believe it is quite possible for us to own a new historical perception and worldview by fully utilizing the characteristics of modern historical studies.

What is called for is for us to overcome the above three faults within the framework of modern historical studies. In chapter 3, we will emphasize the significance of the proposed new world history and, once again, clarify the problems of the present Euro-centric historical view in order to discuss how to be freed from these problems. Furthermore, chapter 3 will also introduce past attempts at forming a new world history and confirm the effectiveness as well as the limitations of these attempts.

CHAPTER 3

ROAD TO
A NEW
WORLD HISTORY

ATTRACTIVENESS OF A NEW WORLD HISTORY

Global Society and a New World History

The standard framework of world history has evolved slowly on a single foundation. Today, however, the limitations of the foundation itself have become obvious, and the framework of world history can no longer respond suitably to movements of the real world. I hope I have convinced readers of this through the preceding two chapters. Today's world is in need of a new world history. What, then, will this new world history be like?

In a nutshell, it is a world history based on earth-centrism for earth inhabitants. And what is earth-centrism? It is the attitude of cherishing the earth on which we live out our lives and attempting to solve the variety of problems occurring on earth—including political, economic, social, and environmental problems—from the viewpoint of global citizens.

Seeing as there is one world and all the people live on the same planet earth, we should be strongly aware of our identity not only as nationals of a particular country but also as members of the global community, or as global citizens. In order for us to act in consideration of the interest of the world as a whole, we need a world perspective that makes us perceive the world not as "our Japan and other countries combined" but as "our one earth."

The new world history should be equipped with contents which, when learned, make us explicitly aware of this world perspective. It is imperative that this world history be something that can convince not only the Japanese—or Westerners, at that—but people all over the world that it is about our own pasts. An ideal world history (1) does not stress differences between oneself and others; (2) does not feature any particular region or country as the center of the world; (3) helps people understand that they are all living together on earth; and (4) makes people realize that all the people in the world have lived together throughout time, being connected with each other.

Is it really possible, one wonders, to create such a new world history?

The majority of those who have engaged in the interpretation and portrayal of history would probably say, "That's a tall order. No chance." This is because, as I pointed out toward the end of chapter 2, almost all of the problems related to the perception of world history in the contemporary world are deeply rooted in the nature of modern historical studies itself. Unless the conventional viewpoint and method of viewing the world are drastically renewed, it would be impossible to attain a new world history. But this does not mean that we should give up on the attempt altogether. That would be the death of historical studies.

Although it has taken too long, we have finally come to be fully aware of the problems with the present world history. Having come this far, then, we must take a new look at the conventional viewpoint on world history understanding and the method of its portrayal, both of which have been uncritically accepted, and advance toward the conception of a new world history. Instead of walking the path that our predecessors had paved, we should change our mindset and boldly forge a new path of our own. There is no need to be afraid of failure. Whether we can create a new world history or not is not the issue. We must create it no matter what.

Tasks for Historians

So that I will not be misunderstood, let me clarify that I am not saying that all those who are interested in historical studies should engage in exploration for a new world history. There is no limit of themes for amateur historians to pursue as personal hobby. They can explore anything that catches their fancy, including their great-grandfather's life, the profile of a city or town 100 years ago, the biography of a foreign hero, the political system of a certain country 300 years ago, deciphering 1,000-year-old documents found in a remote country, the history of their favorite country—and on and on. It is perfectly all right, also, for *rekijo* (female history lovers) to study the lives of feudal warlords of their choice. The new world history that I am proposing is not the only way to approach the past.

It is a different story, however, for professional history researchers like myself who are professionally engaged in historical research in public research institutions, including universities, which are publicly funded. Such researchers should not be allowed to intensively study a particular person's life or read difficult documents from the past simply because they are unique or they seem interesting. That would be no different from a personal hobby. History professionals are required to compile their studies and publish them, and the objectives and significance of their explorations must be clearly stated. History professionals must be explicitly aware of why they find it important to study a particular person, why they read a particular document, what they wish to reveal through their studies, and what meaning their studies have for people in the world.

It is often said that it is sufficient for the studies of individual scholars to be appreciated by fellow scholars in the same field and to have an academic influence on their colleagues. Today, however, what contribution, if any, this academic circle itself makes to society is in question. It is necessary for today's professional historians to constantly and rigorously ask themselves the above questions whenever they set out on a specific study project.

It would be relatively easy, in my judgment, for Japanese history professionals to find meaning in the study of Japanese history. This is because it is only natural for a person who identifies as Japanese to wish to know the past of his/her homeland systematically, just like it is fully understandable if a person wishes to trace his/her own footsteps and understand their significance. The reason for the Japanese government's encouragement of these studies is also easy to understand. But things are not that easy when it comes to studying the history of foreign countries. Why does a Japanese scholar have to study the history of other countries? Why, in most cases, does he publish outcomes of his research in the Japanese language? These are the questions that professional historians in Japan should always be ready to answer. Such a "so-what" attitude as "I am studying the history of this country/region because I like it" is no longer acceptable today in a professional researcher.

Chizuka Tadami was a leading expert in French history who suddenly passed away six months after the publication of his monumental *Shigaku gairon* (Introduction to historical studies)[*20] in the early summer of 2010. In this last work of his, Chizuka declared that the mission of historical studies was to give readers incentive for contemplation. The benefit of historical studies was, he said, the opportunity for readers to deepen their social self-perception. Although it was not written so clearly in the book, it seems that Chizuka wanted to say that studying the history of foreign countries was tantamount to reexamining Japanese history by using other countries' histories as paragons for comparison. But do all scholars in foreign history really carry on their studies with this intention in mind? Actually, it is not so often that Japanese scholars of foreign history speak out regarding interpretations of and views on Japanese history or problems related to today's Japan. To my regret, it is books on the past written by novelists rather than those by scholars in foreign history that exercise greater influence on Japanese people's day-to-day thinking.

Significance of the Study of Foreign History

When I was studying pre-modern Iranian history some time ago, I was bothered by the gap between Iranians' understanding of Iranian history, on the one hand, and the past of the Iranian Plateau that I had understood through my own reading of historical documents in the Persian language, on the other. Iranian people possessed an "our own history" that they believed in, while I had very different views and interpretations. And I wondered, "What's the point of me, a foreigner from Japan, refuting Iranians' understanding of Iranian history and preaching my understanding to them in English or Japanese?"

Close to twenty years ago, when I used to frequent Iran, the question I was asked most often by local people was, "Why are you interested in

---

[*20] Chizuka Tadami, *Shigaku gairon* [Introduction to historical studies] (Tokyo: University of Tokyo Press, 2010).

Iranian history?" This was followed by, "What part of Iranian history are you studying?" I was asked the same questions over and over so often that I had to scream inwardly, "I am just interested in Iranian history, period! It's no one else's business what I study. Why do I have to answer these same questions over and over again? Just leave me alone!"

Iranians are kindhearted people, and they were genuinely pleased to know that a scholar from Japan was interested in the history of their motherland. I wonder, though, if they really understood why a foreigner wanted to study the details of Iranian history. Iranian history is their history, and a foreigner's engagement in it inevitably had to be limited and auxiliary at best.

It is possible for a Japanese scholar of the history of a foreign country to aim at discussing that history on par with historians from that particular country. In fact, there are quite a number of Japanese scholars who have attained that level of excellence in the fields of the histories of Western countries and Chinese history. Efforts by such excellent Japanese scholars of foreign history would be salvaged if the Japanese government generously supported them. But, in actuality, such scholars have to face considerable difficulties. Anywhere in the world, those who study the history of their own country are bound to have a consciousness of "we, the scholars of our own history." How do those Japanese scholars who are not included in this group cope with this consciousness? I wonder if they have any other choice than living in the country, becoming permanent residents there, and, eventually, compiling their findings in the vernacular language.

Even if they do not go that far, they may be able to contribute as a foreigner by pointing out problems from a different angle that local scholars may have overlooked or misunderstood. Even in this case, the Japanese scholars will have to write and speak in that country's language. And, also, the role they play will inevitably be an auxiliary one.

Sometimes, discussion of a certain country's history by a foreign scholar is rationalized as a contribution to the construction of an "objective history" of that country. In this particular case, use of the Japanese language may be justified. But, even in this case, the ultimate goal of this scholar's endeavor can be nothing but assisting in making the present understanding of world history, which is essentially the histories of various countries bound together, more objective. This might have been just fine until today, but such will not be the case from now on. This is because, today, we must conceive a new world history that is not bound by national frameworks. If a conscientious scholar of foreign history continues his study from the same angle with the same method as before, he might fall into an identity crisis.

Attractiveness of a New World History

In contrast, it seems easier for scholars of foreign history to find meaning in conceiving a world history of the global community. This is because this task requires historians to present their interpretations and understandings of the past from the viewpoint of an inhabitant of the earth. As far as this viewpoint is concerned, every historian shares the same position regardless of his/her nationality, whether Japanese, Chinese, or American. Yet, in this task, Japanese historians are denied the privilege of treating Japanese history as something special. This is because the history of the people who live on the Japanese archipelago is a part of the history of inhabitants of the earth. The same thing can be said about the histories of every other country. From this perspective, Japanese scholars' studies of the histories of foreign countries seem quite meaningful. More than that, in fact, Japanese scholars might find themselves in a more advantageous position because they are free from constraints that would have bound historians in that particular country when studying their own national history. Therefore, the world history of the global community is a highly attractive theme for scholars studying the histories of foreign countries.

This new world history has not yet taken a concrete form—which is all the more reason why it is worth taking a crack at. I urge all concerned people to contemplate how to create this new world history. Before that, however, we must acknowledge that a large number of studies aimed at a new world history and their outcomes have been published by historians all over the world who are not content with the framework and interpretation of the present world history. Therefore, the first thing we should do to envision a world history of the global community is to evaluate those existing attempts. Here, let me introduce some of the representative attempts and discuss what aspects should be praised and what aspects are found to be problematic. Also, I intend to explore how to utilize these past attempts to come closer to the realization of a new world history of the global community.

Global History

Before commenting on past attempts at formulating a world history of the global community, let me confirm the relations between a research method called global history and the new world history that I am advocating.

Although it has not really caught on in Japan yet, a research method called global history has been rapidly on the rise in English-speaking countries, including the United States, Britain, and Australia. A good guide to this method available in Japanese is *Gurōbaru hisutorī nyūmon* (Introduction to global history) by Mizushima Tsukasa,[*21] which gives concise explanations of recent developments in this new approach. Because Mizushima's book extensively covers major trends in global history research in Britain and the United States and their findings, I shall refrain from repeating that here. Interested readers are urged to pick up this book.

The term "global history" has been used in various occasions with a variety of meanings, and it defies easy definition. According to Mizushima, global history has the following five characteristics:

1. Extensive length of the time period it covers. Global history applies a macroscopic view on history;

---

*21 Mizushima Tsukasa, *Gurōbaru hisutorī nyūmon* [Introduction to global history] (Tokyo: Yamakawa Shuppansha, 2010).

2. Wide variety of themes to be addressed as well as vast expansion of the space it covers;

3. Relativization of the European world and relativization of history after the modern age;

4. Emphasis on interrelations and mutual influences between different regions; and

5. Novelty of research objects and themes.

Actually, the world history of the global community that I advocate shares these characteristics in many respects. Sharing an aim to grasp the history of humankind on a global scale, it can be said that these two histories basically belong to the same research genre. In fact, I have already learned a lot from the fruits of global history studies in English-speaking countries. And I am determined to keep close watch on its development.

Nevertheless, as I will criticize this school below, quoting several concrete examples, many results of global history research have inherited the conventional worldview and history perception of the English-speaking sphere without modification. For this reason, I do not always find them acceptable. In the Western world, until quite recently, the pasts of Europe and non-Europe have been discussed separately within different academic frameworks of historical studies and Oriental studies, respectively. In other words, these two were not regarded as research fields belonging to the same category. For this reason, the idea of combining European history and non-European history together, which is already commonsensical in Japan, tends to appear as something novel in the eyes of scholars in the Western world. Sometimes, when non-European history, such as Asian history, is simply added to European history, which retains its conventional interpretations, this is regarded as a global history.

Also, some argue that global history is not the history of humankind on a global scale but a portrayal of the process of economic unification of a world that had originally been fragmented. This is not what I have in mind as the new world history.

Therefore, let me warn readers that adopting the research method of global history will not automatically lead to a new world history. In order to conceive a world history of the global community, a new world-view and a new historical perception are indispensable. Global history unaccompanied by these is nothing but an epigone of the present world history.

OVERCOMING THE EURO-CENTRIC HISTORICAL VIEW

Two Centers

As I discussed toward the end of chapter 2, the present world history has three faults. Once these three are overcome, we will have a new world history. A number of attempts have been made so far to overcome these three faults, which can be roughly divided into two categories: (1) elimination of centricity and (2) discovery of mutual relationship. From the outset of this section, I'd like to explain what "centricity" in the historical view is all about and how it can be overcome. Subsequently, I intend to introduce the major research attempts made so far in the aforementioned two categories and follow that up with discussion on their significance and limitations.

First, what is the nature of this thing called "historical view centered around xxx (a specific country/region)" and how can it be overcome? One may have to be careful when referring to "centricity," because, strictly speaking, there are two types of centricity. When one stands on a specific spot on earth and portrays world history as centered on that particular location, there is an issue of centricity. The notion that a specific group of people or a specific region is considered to have moved world history is another manifestation of centricity. The former type of centricity is found in attempts to interpret world history as centered around, for instance, Japan, while the view that Europe has been the prime mover of world history is a typical example of the second type.

The former type of centricity is viable even when the latter type of centricity is adopted. For example, it is possible to conceive world history as centered around Japan in the recognition that it is Europe that has moved world history. The Euro-centric historical view has both of the two characteristics—that is, it places Europe in the center of world history (former type of centricity) and believes that Europe has led world history (latter type).

Of the two, the latter type is particularly problematic for understanding and portraying world history. Adopting this position is tantamount to agreeing that only a portion of people on earth created the structure of world history, which inevitably leads to acceptance of the dichotomous worldview that world history consists of a center and a periphery. The world history of the global community that I advocate takes the view that today's world has been created by the total sum of activities of all the people in the world, not by a specific group of people. The new world history, therefore, will have to free itself not only from the Euro-centric historical view but also from all other kinds of "xxxx-centric" historical views. Supposition of a center automatically leads to supposition of a periphery, which is no different from the present dichotomous view of world history.

Euro-Centric Historical View

The greatest problem inherent in the present view on world history in today's Japan is its Euro-centric orientation. Even though this has long been pointed out, the view that world history has revolved around Europe is hard to shake off. How will we be able to overcome this "disease"? Let us start our discussion with this question.

From the observations we made in chapter 2, we are already aware of an effective remedy for this ailment. It is to perceive the pasts by demarcating "Europe" as a concept separate from Europe as a geographical space.

The history of "Europe" as a concept, which encompasses all the positive values, is characterized by its tendency to take in and piece together the histories of various regions in Europe as geographical spaces as needed and to narrate and portray Europe as if it had a consistent history. It is imperative to become fully aware of the artificiality of such explanations and descriptions and to criticize and dissolve the history of "Europe" as a concept.

After dissolution of the history of "Europe" as a concept, there should remain the pasts of Europe as a geographical space and the people who have lived there. But these pasts are not concluded within this geographical space alone. They interacted closely with the pasts of the people in such regions as central Eurasia and northern Africa. The migration of various Germanic peoples occurred as part of the migration of people from central Eurasia, and some Germanic peoples crossed the Strait of Gibraltar and settled in northern Africa. Christianity, which is strongly related to "Europe" as a concept, was not born in Europe as a geographical space. It is also obvious that the southeastern part of Europe as a geographical space was ruled over for hundreds of years by the Ottoman Empire, a political power that had been excluded from "Europe."

Given these facts, it is almost meaningless to concentrate on Europe as a geographical space in discussing European history. In discussing the pasts of this region of the world, it is, in my judgment, better to use a more neutral term, such as west Eurasia, which vaguely refers to the western part of the Eurasian continent landmass, instead of Europe, which is geographically limited to the landmass west of the Ural Mountains. Here, Let us ignore the fact that the term Eurasia was invented by combining Europe and Asia, and, thus, it would be appropriate not to use it. As long as one frees oneself from "Europe" as a concept, there is no need to use such a trite term as Europe when thinking about world history.

I must admit my suggestion might sound extremely radical. To prevent unnecessary misunderstanding, let me clarify that I am not saying that we should not use the term "Europe" in portraying world history. The new world history that I am advocating must by all means include an explanation about the emergence of "Europe" as a value or a concept as well as the past and present presence of the people who believe that they belong to this geographical space. It should also discuss how the convictions and behaviors of the dwellers of Europe have greatly influenced the lives of all the people on earth, including those who live in Europe as a geographical space. If one feels uncomfortable using such an unfamiliar geographical term as west Eurasia, then use of the term Europe should be permissible as long as it is clear that the term denotes a geographical space. Specifying whether the term refers to northwestern Europe or eastern Europe, for example, would clarify matters.

What I am criticizing is the attitude that presupposes the existence of a unified historical space called Europe and discusses history only within that framework. I am also critical of the perception that Europe is an existing historical space that is demarcated from others in world history. It is this attitude and perception that has substantiated "Europe" as a concept and nurtured the dichotomous view of world history.

It is their privilege and well within their discretion for people who feel a sense of belonging to the European Union (EU), an actual political and economic union, to portray its history. As a matter of fact, such a project is being conducted with the purpose of consolidating the EU's political foundation, and the possibility of compiling a common history textbook for its member countries has actually been explored. Utmost caution must be paid to ensure, though, that such a textbook does not become another history of "Europe" as a concept.

Examination of World History Textbooks

Before I elaborate on my proposals, let me point out the problems of the present world history in concrete terms. How have the histories of "Europe" as a concept and as a geographical space been intermingled? To illustrate my point, let us again consider the aforementioned *Shōsetsu sekaishi B* (Detailed account of world history B), particularly its chapter 9 on the birth of modern Europe. Page 187 of the said chapter reads:

> With the arrival of the Age of Discovery, unification of the world commenced. European commerce began to spread worldwide: commodities diversified and trade values expanded. At the same

time, the center of Europe's long-distance trade shifted from the Mediterranean to countries along the Atlantic Ocean (the period of the Commercial Revolution). Formation of a global commercial sphere led to the opening of vast overseas markets and facilitated the development of a capitalistic economy, which had already been in the embryonic stage. The massive inflow of silver from Latin American silver mines, including the Potosi silver mine discovered in 1545, doubled or even tripled commodity prices in Europe. This high rate of inflation has come to be called the price revolution. The price revolution was a grave blow to feudal lords, who depended on income from rent for living.

While commerce and industry became increasingly vigorous in west European countries, manorialism (*Gutsherrschaft*), in which feudal lords managed land under their direct holdings to produce grains for export, became rampant in Europe east of the Elbe to meet the increasing demand for grains from Western European countries. This further strengthened feudal lords' rule over serfs. The establishment of this division of labor between the east and the west had significant influences on subsequent developments in Eastern Europe.[*22]

Although it was about developments inside "Europe" instead of the entire world, this quote talks about the shift of the center of long-distance trade. At the back of this description is the understanding that Europe is a self-contained space clearly demarcated from other spaces (i.e., demarcation between oneself and others). This can be verified by the statement, "Massive inflow of silver from Latin American silver mines ... doubled or even tripled commodity prices in Europe" in the middle of the first paragraph. But, let us pause and think here. Was it really throughout the entirety of Europe as a geographical space that the development of a capitalist economy occurred and the price revolution

---

[*22] Satō Tsugitaka, et al., *Shōsetsu sekaishi B* [Detailed account of world history B] (Tokyo: Yamakawa Shuppansha, 2007), 187.

delivered serious blows to feudal lords? If that was indeed so, why did a discrepancy in conditions emerge between Eastern and Western Europe as the paragraph continued to describe? It is hard to imagine that the aforementioned incidents actually did take place commonly throughout the entirety of Europe as a geographical space. Such developments as the development of capitalism, price inflation, and blows incurred by feudal lords must have been phenomena seen only in a portion of Europe as a geographical space. In that sense, this particular portion of the textbook does not describe the history of Europe as a geographical space. It is the history of "Europe" as a concept that was inserted to explain the later development of capitalism.

Another important observation is the total absence of reference to the economic and social conditions of Latin America, where the Potosi silver mine was located, or Asia, which must have been connected to Lisbon as a part of the global commercial sphere. The quoted paragraph reads as if everything had taken place and evolved only within Europe. While establishment of the global commercial sphere must have been accomplished through close interactions with non-European regions, the paragraph only talks about the impact that it had on "Europe" (i.e., development of a capitalistic economy). One may wonder, for instance, if price hikes did not take place in regions other than Europe, or if there was no change in the feudal lord system in non-European regions. Reading these paragraphs uncritically, one gets the impression that non-European regions made no initiative and that only Europe moved history. This is a typical manifestation of the Euro-centric historical view.

If various regions of the world are connected with each other through trade, there should necessarily be interrelatedness and interconnectedness among economies and cultural happenings in various regions of the world. If the habit of concentrating descriptions on a region that is deemed to be the center can be overcome, it becomes possible to grasp the interrelatedness of happenings as a whole and describe how things become interconnected across regions and cultural spheres as they evolve. This is what deserves to be called a new world history. The most important thing is how to set ourselves free from the conventional interpretation of history centered around "Europe" as a concept, which takes a framework called Europe as a prerequisite.

In order to overcome the Euro-centric historical view, we must undertake steady efforts to thoroughly scrutinize all the popular theories of European history to (1) distinguish phenomena that are related to "Europe" as a concept and those that are pertinent to geographical Europe and (2) discard, in principle, all the phenomena related to "Europe" as a concept and verify how phenomena pertinent to geographical Europe are related to phenomena in peripheral regions beyond the boundary.

TO OVERCOME OTHER "*XXXX*-CENTRIC" HISTORICAL VIEWS

The Islamic-Centric Historical View

The Euro-centric historical view is not the only problematic understanding of the past. The history of the "Islamic world", which was established in the nineteenth century as a spatial concept in juxtaposition with "Europe," is equally problematic. In today's Japan, the Islamic world is understood to be a world in which all the occurrences in it can be explained with the characteristics of Islam. In contrast to Europe, which can be envisioned as a space defined by a geographical framework, the Islamic world as it is addressed in high school textbooks in Japan alters its spatial size in different eras; therefore, it is more difficult to deal with (see fig. 5). Moreover, whether a region is called an Islamic world or not depends on the extremely simple standard of whether its ruler is Muslim or not. The standard is based on the premise that a Muslim ruler must govern in the Islamic way and that that Islamic way is significantly different from other regions.

Why, then, has the history of such a peculiar space that exists on a dichotomous understanding (i.e., Islamic vs. non-Islamic) gained entry in world history as if its existence were merely natural? Because it takes a long explanation to answer this question, interested readers

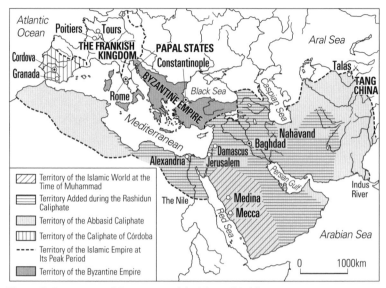

Figure 5. Expansion and Contraction of the Islamic World

In this map, geographic spaces ruled by Muslim regimes are understood to constitute the Islamic world.

SOURCE: "Sekai no rekishi" Henshū Iinkai, ed., *Mō ichido yomu Yamakawa sekaishi* [Yamakawa's world history revisited] (Tokyo: Yamakawa Shuppansha, 2009).

are encouraged to pick up my 2005 book *Isuramu sekai no sōzō* (Creating the notion of the Islamic world).[*23] In any event, there is no space in the new world history that I am proposing for this kind of spatial setting that demarcates itself from others.

So that I will not be misunderstood, let me say that people who have a sense of belonging to or who feel an affinity toward the Islamic world as a spatial concept are at liberty to portray the history of the Islamic world centered around the Islamic religion, like in the case of the European Union. But, again, just like in the case of Europe, it would be utterly impossible to portray a world history that advocates that there

---

*23 Haneda Masashi, *Isuramu sekai no sōzō* [Creating the notion of the Islamic world] (Tokyo: University of Tokyo Press, 2005).

is one world while retaining the concept of an Islamic world demarcated from the rest of the world.

What, then, should be done with the historical description that is today labeled Islamic world history? The answer is very simple. All we need to do is remove the framework "Islamic world" from it. Because of this framework, it is often considered that an Islamic nature should exist inside this world, which is different from the non-Islamic world. Sometimes, it is even insisted that Islam was the center of world history and that it was Islam that created the modern world. It is explained that at a certain point, the center of this world shifted from Baghdad to Cairo. These statements share the same structure that is found in the discussion of "Europe" as a concept. All we need to do is to stop demarcating between the Islamic world and the non-Islamic world. The first step is to reexamine the discourse that has been narrated as Islamic world history. And when we do so, we need to pay more attention to connections and commonalities with neighboring regions so as to avoid isolating the Islamic world as a self-contained unit.

Exploration of Commonalities and Relationship

It is often explained that migration within the Islamic world was easy and frequent because people shared Islamic law and Arabic language. In pre-modern times, however, rampant migration was not confined to the Islamic world. Jews and members of the Armenian Apostolic Church also moved around frequently throughout the wide expanse of land, while the Sogdian people used to come and go on the Silk Road in central Eurasia. Thus, the above statement about migration within the Islamic world needs to be reexamined, taking into consideration the migrations of other, non-Muslim people.

A number of recent studies claim that Islamic law was adopted to rule society in all the regions where the Islamic religion was widespread. According to these studies, this is a proof that the concept of the Islamic world is valid. Indeed, this statement is valid and correct from the viewpoint of those who wish to use the Islamic world concept proactively. It would be effective to emphasize the importance of the Islamic law when writing an Islamic world history.

It would do more harm than good, however, to stress the uniqueness of Islamic law in a world history of the global community. For one thing, even in a society whose ruler was Muslim, more often than not a feudal lord's own laws and judgments—which were rooted in common law not directly related to Islamic law—played an important role. Thus, it is wrong to think that it was only Islamic law that ruled these societies. Also, it should be noted that most texts of Islamic law were actually commandments that Muslims were expected to comply with and guidelines for a religiously correct life. This kind of law is found not only in Islam but also in Christianity, Judaism, Buddhism, and Confucianism. In fact, it is fairly common among religions. It is not correct to say that Islam as a religion and Islamic law were exceptional. In the new world history, even as differences among religions are recognized, the commonalities among them should be emphasized.

Seen from the viewpoint of comparison with other regions and relations with them, a lot of unknowns still remain about the history of West Asia, which is the center of the Islamic world. For example, when commodity prices doubled or tripled somewhere in Europe, or when feudal lords' right to rule became shaky, how much was West Asia affected, given its close economic relations with various regions of Europe through trade via the Mediterranean and the sea route around the Cape of Good Hope? What were the family relations and social division of labor between men and women in West Asia? What are the commonalities and differences with other regions of the world?

As I have argued elsewhere, in international trade, the political authorities of the Iranian Plateau treated the British and Dutch East India Companies, aliens to them and Christians, better than they treated Iranian and Turkic merchants, who were Muslims and "one of us" to them. This puzzles people and makes them wonder why. Wasn't the capitulation system that established the basis for extraterritorial privileges (freedom of trade and residence, consular court, etc.) that the Ottoman Empire granted European countries based on the same idea?

These are just a few examples of countless questions on past research findings and issues to be clarified from now on.

To repeat myself once again, the most important thing is to lift the spatial restriction of the Islamic world first and reexamine the past of Eurasia as a whole once again, paying special attention to the commonalities and relations among the various actors. The history of West Asia, which is located in the center of Eurasia, occupies a particularly important position when conceiving a new world history that takes note of the interconnectedness of the human community as a whole.

Sino-Centric Historical View

When one tries to explore the origin of a contemporary state or a region by going back in time, there is a tendency to fall into a group-centric historical view. China is no exception. In Chinese history, whenever a great dynastic polity, such as Han and Tang, was established, it was considered an era of integration; all the other periods of history were regarded as eras of disunity. Hidden in this view is a value judgment that says that the vast Chinese continent must have been politically unified from the very beginning. This historical understanding would be a natural outcome when one projects conditions of the late Qing dynasty and of modern to contemporary China on the entire past of this vast space, making one believe that China must always have existed. But if this vast space, which was no smaller than all of Europe, was actually politically unified, given the incomparably rudimentary level of transportation and communications in the pre-modern period, it must have been an exceptional accomplishment.

The environments and human habitat conditions differed significantly between dry, wheat-growing North China and humid, rice-growing South China. The same thing can be said of the coastal regions of Central and South China and the inland upstream of the Yellow River in the northwest. It is true that major dynastic polities had rituals and institutions that had been passed on for generations that were, in principle, adopted by succeeding dynasties at the time of dynastic transition.

Because the succeeding dynasty was mandated to record the history of the preceding dynasty, the continuity of history is undeniable at least on the dynastic level. Nevertheless, it was a view of the pasts centered around dynasties' political history and which relied on a blind acceptance of descriptions found in history books written by writers who had had a strong sense of belonging to these dynasties. Once freed from this dynastic history context, the history of the Chinese continent might become significantly different from how it is understood today.

Another problem inherent in Chinese history is its Han race–centric historical view—that is, the belief that Chinese history has evolved as the history of the Han race, which had existed from the distant past. According to this historical view, for instance, the Yuan dynasty established by Mongols and the Manchu-led Qing dynasty are seen as dynasties of conquerors. The question remains, however, how much compatriot consciousness was shared by pre-modern people in "China" who spoke different languages in different regions even under the rule of the same political authority. This seems to be an issue that is worth examining again.

Demarcation between *hua* ("civilized") and *yi* ("barbarians") is a theme that has been much discussed not only in China itself but also among intellectuals on the Korean Peninsula and the Japanese archipelago, both of which experienced heavy cultural influences from China. It should be noted that this is a view of the world that basically shares the same structure as the Euro-centric historical view that we have made an issue of here. While a new world history should take note of the presence of people with this kind of view in China, like in Europe, who influenced actual trends in politics, narrating Chinese history in line with this view should be avoided.

As we have seen so far, the pasts of the Chinese continent seem to be bound by three elements: China, dynasties, and the Han race. As in the case of Europe, it is advisable to avoid the use of "China" as a geographical term as much as possible when discussing the pasts of China and its peripheries and, instead, resort to a neutral term such as eastern Eurasia. And I'd like to suggest that scholars of eastern Eurasian history should dismantle such traditional frameworks of historical description as China, dynasties, and the Han race, and have another look at the history of this region, paying attention to relations with neighboring regions.

Recently, voices suggesting revision of the Sino-centric historical view from the viewpoint of Central Eurasia have become quite powerful. It is certainly important to free the pasts of the Central Eurasian nomads, non-Chinese tribes located in northern China and often looked down on as barbarians, from the Sino-centric historical interpretations. When the history of a certain region or group of people is reviewed from a previously untested angle, often a different historical understanding emerges.

But if this revision leads to the creation of a Central Eurasia–centric world history—that is, a historical view that Central Eurasia was the center and the prime mover of world history—such would nullify my offered opinion. It is beyond doubt that nomads in Central Eurasia played an important role in distributing people, goods, and information to various regions in Eurasia. Nevertheless, to place these nomads in the center of world history is completely different from the attempt to realize a world history of the global community that aims at eliminating any particular centricity from historical view.

Japan-Centric Historical View

Minamizuka Shingo, in his provocatively titled book *Sekaishi nante iranai?* (We don't need world history, do we?),[*24] pointed out that, now that problems contemporary Japan faces have become globalized beyond regional and temporal frameworks, historical thinking, too, should be nurtured on a global scale. Minamizuka argues that, in order to cope with today's problems, it is necessary to create a world history that incorporates Japanese history or a Japanese history paying close attention to world history. I agree with the basic direction of Minamizuka's

---

*24 Minamizuka Shingo, *Sekaishi nante iranai?* [We don't need world history, do we?] (Tokyo: Iwanami Shoten, 2007).

argument. What comes to mind first when hearing the term Japanese history, however, is a single country's history to interpret and describe the past of people in and around the Japanese archipelago. This single country history is, so to speak, in a tube, separated from the pasts of other geographical spaces. If we accept this kind of Japanese history, then we should also accept such clusters as Korean history, Chinese history, and French history in world history—which would be no different from the structure of the present world history.

For Japanese, this tube-like narrative of Japanese history has an important role to play in strengthening their identity as people sharing a common past. Depriving Japanese of this Japanese history would, therefore, weaken their sense of belonging to Japan. In that sense, I believe the present basic framework of Japanese history should be maintained as long as Japan exists as a country. Of course, it cannot be a completely one-country history, and there should be plenty of room for revisions, taking into consideration the pasts of neighboring regions. Nevertheless, it should be permissible to retain a Japanese history that is seen from the point of view of the Japanese archipelago and written solely for the Japanese people. This is a Japanese history not for the purpose of generating parochial nationalism but for the purpose of raising the Japanese consciousness of Japan as one of multiple sources of their sense of belonging. Because Japan does exist as a country, the Japanese should remain both Japanese nationals and global citizens at the same time, at least for the time being.

On the other hand, the new world history is for us to obtain an identity as global citizens. As such, there is no particular need for Japanese history in it. Of course, there should be plenty of references to Japan and the Japanese in the new world history. But such references should be made from a different angle than that of the conventional Japanese history contained in a tube. Japanese history should be compatible with the new world history.

To illustrate this point, let's posit that citizenship of Nagasaki prefecture is compatible with Japanese nationality, and the history of Nagasaki prefecture is compatible with Japanese history. The history of Nagasaki is by no means included within Japanese history like a tube separated from others. Instead, Nagasaki is referred to only from time to time. Perhaps the relationship between Japanese history and the new world history will be something similar to this.

CENTER AND PERIPHERY

World-Systems Theory

Eliminating centricity from world history goes completely against the argument of Immanuel Wallerstein's world-systems theory. Wallerstein's theory has exercised great influence on the understanding of world history in Japan since the 1980s. Let us look into this issue.

For clarity, let me begin by summarizing the major points of this world-systems theory. Wallerstein argues that a unitary economic sphere encompassing Europe and the Americas had been formed by the seventeenth century through the activities of "Europeans." He names this economic structure, which had not existed previously, a "modern world system." Regions incorporated into this system could not remain economically independent, and each one produced commodities in accordance with a system-wide division of labor. Inside the system, regions were divided into core countries, semi-periphery countries, and periphery countries. The core countries exercised economic hegemony over other regions. The Netherlands was the core country in the seventeenth century, succeeded by Britain in the mid-eighteenth through nineteenth centuries, and by the United States in the twentieth century. The core countries where production capacity was increased by mechanization produced sophisticated industrial products and received supplies of raw materials and food from the peripheries. Consequently, the structure for the core countries to exploit the peripheries was perpetuated; wealth accumulated in the core countries while the peripheries became increasingly impoverished. This modern world system was fundamentally different from previous social structures because cultural and political unity was absent there. Instead, the logic that maintained its coherence was capitalistic economy.

In summary, Wallerstein argues that the world system that had emerged in a part of geographical Europe swallowed up other regions in the world one after another until the system encompassed the entire globe. And this system was characterized by the capitalistic division of labor among member regions and the political and cultural disunity among them.

This is a very well thought out and powerfully influential view on the past. In actuality, the contemporary world is not unified politically and culturally, but it can be seen as being integrated economically. It appears that the world-systems theory has, to a certain extent, succeeded in convincingly explaining how this economic unity came about and why the disparity of wealth emerged among various regions. But, for the following two reasons, I do not think this theory can be called a world history of the global community.

First, the view advocated by this world-systems theory is extremely close to the Euro-centric historical view. The world historical view advocated by Wallerstein's theory claims that today's globalized world system is an expansion and extension of the system established in Europe in the sixteenth century. When it is explained that a world system was born first and that it continued to expand by swallowing neighboring regions, people may be led to understand that only the world system moved proactively and its peripheries just passively reacted to the world system's initiatives. In short, this explanation draws a picture of one actor moving of its own volition and another actor lacking a will of its own, and thus merely being co-opted by the former. The Euro-centric historical view narrates that "Europe" moved to create history while non-Europe had no history. It is obvious that these two narratives share a common perspective on the past.

Second, the view that the world is made of core countries and periphery countries goes against the direction that a new world history would take to eliminate any centricity. As I have repeatedly pointed out, the present world history tends to narrate history around a center somewhere in the world, be it political, economic, or cultural. In this sense, the world-systems theory shares an identical characteristic with the present world history.

No Need for a Center

Why does the world need a center in the first place? It seems true that wealth is maldistributed in today's world. Huge gaps in political power and military might also exist among countries. When the United States and Angola in Africa are compared, for instance, the difference in the impact on world politics and economy between the two is unmistakable. Nonetheless, should we, as citizens of the contemporary world, declare that the United States is the center of the world and Angola a peripheral country? Such understanding would emphasize the differences between the United States and Angola and hamper the development of a common sense of belonging to the same earth among peoples in these two countries.

A new world history that aims to promote the perception that there is one world must free itself from this very understanding. All the movements in the world are connected with each other. If a phenomenon that could be labeled capitalism did indeed emerge first in a part of geographical Europe, it was by no means created by activities of people in that particular region alone. It should be perceived, instead, that the mutually interrelated activities of people all over the world resonated with each other to result in the establishment of capitalism in a particular place on earth, while other phenomena (e.g., intensive production of certain commodities or mass-migration of people) emerged in other regions. It is one single phenomenon overall, but it projects different images depending on what one pays attention to. It is, if you will, like the Buddhist statue of Ashura with three heads with three faces each and either four or six arms, or the eleven-faced statue of the Goddess of Kannon.

It is true today that capitalistic ideas provide the foundations of economic activities in a number of regions in the world. Traditionally, it has been interpreted that these ideas were given to those regions or forced on them by the West since the nineteenth century. Seen from a different angle, however, it may be said that people in various regions of the world, having realized the merits of capitalism in the West, either modified similar institutions which had existed in their own regions or adopted capitalistic ideas after localizing them to fit their society according to their own will. As a matter of fact, even though they are all clustered under the name of capitalism, the realities of the economic activities of various countries in the contemporary world are quite diverse. It would be too one-sided to hold the view, as world-systems theory argues, that non-Europe became subsumed into the world (or economy) centered around a part of "Europe" through the medium of capitalism.

I am of the view that it is not always necessary to designate a center when describing the history of the world of the past. From the viewpoint of economic history, it is understandable that people wish to know what or who is moving the economy. Once we are set free from the notions that the economy is at the base of all of people's life and that the trend of world history can be explained in a coherent and regular manner by concentrating on economics, however, there will be no significant meaning in discussing what the center is.

If a "center" must be discussed, it should be noted that the center in religious and spiritual worldviews must have had a more important and more poignant meaning for people, particularly in the pre-modern period. Christians in west Eurasia, for instance, believed Jerusalem to be the center of the world. Devout Muslims would have posited Mecca in the center of the world. It is well known that Chinese empires regarded where their emperors resided as the center of the world. That countries in the world were loosely connected economically but people in each region lived their own lives with respective worldviews and their own "we are the center" consciousness may be closer to people's day-to-day image of the world.

From the Periphery's Perspective

On the flipside of the elimination of centricity from world history is a method for seeing world history from the periphery's perspective. This method is an attempt to reexamine world history as a whole from the perspective of the periphery rather than from the center as the present world historical view does. By viewing world history from the periphery, it is hoped that contradictions and fallacies in the present view from the center can be uncovered.

One of the examples toward this direction is the attempt made by historians who question the Euro-centric historical view to criticize the said historical view by putting other regions such as Asia and Africa at the center instead. The attempts at interpreting world history from the Islamic world-centric position pursued by such scholars of the Islamic world as Itagaki Yūzō, Miki Wataru, and Gotō Akira since the 1970s have become considerably influential today and have been effective in exposing the fictive nature of the interpretations of the Euro-centric world history.

A similar attempt has also been made regarding the Sino-centric historical view. Representative of this attempt are approaches taken by Okada Hidehiro and Sugiyama Masaaki to look anew at Chinese history from the aforementioned Central Eurasian perspective. The National Institute for Advanced Humanistic Studies at Fudan University in Shanghai is conducting the Viewing China from the Periphery research project as one of four research projects conducted under the leadership of its director Ge Zhaoguang, a leading Chinese humanities scholar. It is particularly noteworthy that it is Chinese scholars themselves who are trying to reexamine the centricity of China as a concept.

If these and other attempts lead to the revision and relativization of the historical view centered around a particular region (e.g., the Euro-centric historical view), such should be welcomed in principle. Nevertheless, we must be cautious of a liability in the method: viewing history from the periphery can lead to envisioning a world history centered around the periphery itself. For instance, *Reorient: Global Economy* *in the Asian Age*[*25] by Andre Frank, one of the representative advocates of global history research, strongly impacted readers worldwide by attacking the Euro-centric historical view and pointing out that the center of the world economy has always been Asia except for the brief period since the nineteenth century in which Europe became dominant. The book predicts that the age of Asia, which has been regarded as a periphery in recent years, will come soon. Seen from Japanese eyes, the argument of this book plays on our ego as Asians and makes us want to shout with exultation. Anyone who reads this book, however, finds its descriptions to be too favorable to Asia, aiming to denounce the Euro-centric historical view. In my judgment, the book is on the level of an Asia-centric argument.

While this method to view the center from the periphery should be encouraged as a means to criticize existing historical views, it would be difficult to construct a new world history with this method alone. The intention to view from the periphery is itself the intention to view from the center inverted. From now on, we need to incorporate images seen from both the periphery and the center and create a perspective on world history that does not have a center or a periphery.

Gender and Subaltern

Eliminating centricity from historical descriptions is not confined to rejecting a conceptual center like "Europe." Some historians criticized the discipline's (which included themselves) lopsided attention in the nineteenth century through the first half of the twentieth century on the nation-state, white males, and political history. Based on this, studies on a variety of peripheries including females, children, diasporas, and other elements that are bound to be dropped from the framework of the nation-state have been vigorously conducted by scholars, including, most notably, those who belong to the Annales School in France. The rise of social history research in Japan in the 1980s may have something

---

*25 Andre Frank, *Reorient: Global Economy in the Asian Age* (Berkeley: University of California Press, 1998).

to do with this trend. Historical research focusing on gender, which has become quite widespread recently, is also something to be watched closely as a rebellion toward the present male-centric historical interpretations and descriptions that have turned a blind eye to women, who make up 50 percent of the entire population of the world.

Yet an attempt at narrating world history by focusing solely on women is liable to fall into a female-centric historical view. Women's history should exist as an independent field of research. By way of how it relates with a new world history, the history of women should focus on correcting the commonly accepted male-centric historical view by reviewing the past from a more female perspective, and describing history thus. This can help people understand the roles and positions of men and women in society.

As an example of attempts at focusing on peripheries in historical understanding, let me introduce a research method that pays special attention to a group of people called the subaltern. The method was first advocated in the 1980s in the area of South Asian history and later became well known throughout the world. Scholars who adopted this method in the 1980s found that traditional South Indian historical research had merely followed the viewpoints of the colonial rulers in terms of understanding and description. They criticized that this traditional approach was inadequate from the viewpoint of the subalterns (here meaning the colonized people, who, because they were colonized, were considered to belong to a lower strata of society). The scholars stressed the importance of viewing history from the viewpoint of silent, marginalized but common people.

While this proposal subsequently became a major trend, spilling over to Latin American studies and others, some scholars, including Gayatri Spivak, started criticizing the arbitrariness of the method as a way to understand the world and people through the eyes of modern Western knowledge. Spivak insisted that this group of people, the subaltern, had been "created" by modern Western knowledge; it could be understood only when narrated in the manner of modern Western knowledge; and that the subalterns did not have a means to talk about themselves. In a nutshell, she claimed that the very act of talking about the subaltern is an exercise of modern Western knowledge's power to interpret the world for its convenience.

Historians try to interpret and understand the past on the basis of available historical documents and narrate history in their own words. According to Spivak, this behavior itself is an exercise of power not only toward the subaltern but also toward the non-subaltern as well as all the people in the past who had recorded historical documents. Although Spivak did not criticize specific methods of historical research directly, I believe all historians must humbly pay attention to her criticisms.

Nevertheless, I do not take a position that the presence of historical studies itself should be denied. As long as people wish to know the past, they should be allowed to make attempts at approaching the past in one way or another. And historical studies are currently the most effective means available for people to realize this wish. The question is how to use this means. Historians are urged to use historical documents more prudently when approaching the past, fully aware of the meaning as well as the impact on all quarters of their own research and description of history. The conception of a new world history devoid of any centricity would be a good laboratory for this exercise.

Potential of an Environmental History

As an object of modern historical research since the nineteenth century, the environment has undoubtedly remained in the periphery for a long time. Only recently has research on political, socio-economic, or cultural histories paid adequate attention to environmental factors. Disputes over natural resources, including agricultural, forestry, and mining products, have broken out all over the world since ancient times, but they have been interpreted almost exclusively in the context of political or military histories. An analysis from the viewpoint of the environment was hardly seen until about twenty years ago. While references were occasionally made to epidemics or climate change, they have not necessarily been recognized as factors that could greatly move history.

Today, however, when environmental issues have become a serious problem on a global scale and people have begun to seriously discuss how human beings should coexist with the earth's environment, people have naturally become more interested in past relations between humankind and the environment. "Environment" in this case is not confined to themes directly concerned with relations between human beings and the environment, such as the environmental devastation. The term also encompasses a variety of issues including land use, demography, and development.

Needless to say, the environment has exerted truly profound influences on the history of humankind. For example, although accurate statistics are not available, it is estimated that about one-third of the Eurasian population perished in the outbreak of the plague in the mid-fourteenth century. It is said that western Eurasia lost so many peasants that feudal lords were forced to concede to the demands of peasants in order to secure enough manpower. This incident is considered to have triggered the collapse of the prevalent social order of the times known as feudalism.

When the Spaniards advanced into the Americas in the late fifteenth to sixteenth centuries, pathogenic bacteria of Eurasian origin also crossed the Atlantic. These germs caused numerous outbreaks of epidemics, including smallpox, typhoid, and influenza, among local people who had not been immune to those germs. Some argue that close to 95 percent of the pre-Columbian population of the Americas was lost to these epidemics. American natives had already been defeated by bacteria before they lost battles with the Spaniards.

It is obvious from these examples that the environment has undoubtedly been a major factor that moved world history. But it wasn't until relatively recently that several historians became aware of it. Since then, studies on environmental history have become rapidly invigorated.

Guns, Germs, and Steel: The Fates of Human Societies[26] written

---

[26] Jared Diamond, *Guns, Germs, and Steel: The Fates of Human Societies* (New York: W. W. Norton, 1997).

by Jared Diamond, an American ecologist, geographer, biologist, and anthropologist, is not only an outstanding academic achievement in the field of environmental history but also masterpiece reading. Diamond questions why the Eurasian people went and conquered the Americas instead of the North and South Americans heading to Eurasia. This is a grandiose question that region- or country-locked historians would never have come up with. The wide variety of arguments employed to answer this question are indisputably intriguing. It was after I read the Japanese translation of this book (published in 2000) that I belatedly became aware of the importance of environmental history. The abundant potentiality of environmental history is clearly demonstrated by this book. As Diamond himself proved, highly original and meaningful findings would certainly emerge if historians utilized the products of scientific research in, say, physiology or biogeography or conducted joint research with researchers in those fields.

When I revisited Diamond's book recently, however, I became aware of a critical defect of this otherwise wonderful book. When discussing the past of humankind, Diamond uncritically used names of groups of people and historical spaces that are employed in the present world history. A typical manifestation of this is his use of "Europe" and "European(s)." Also, he failed to distinguish Europe as a geographical space and "Europe" as a concept. Furthermore, he understood the flow of world history as a competition toward a common goal among numerous groups of people on earth. Thus, Diamond says:

A historian who had lived at any time between 8500 BCE and 1450 CE, and who had tried then to predict future historical trajectories, would surely have labeled Europe's eventual dominance as the least likely outcome, because Europe was the most backward of those three Old World regions for most of those 10,000 years.[27]

*27 Ibid., 409.

He closed this colossal work with the following question, "Why, then, did ... China eventually lose their enormous leads of thousands of years to late-starting Europe?"[*28]

The historical view that Diamond shared with readers, such as the progression of history, the existence of several different cultural spheres, and among those cultural spheres, the progressiveness of Europe, is essentially the same as the understanding of world history currently prevalent in Japan. In Diamond's work, the core of the interpretation of world history that is prevalent today is preserved unmodified. Diamond's book is truly outstanding in paying special attention to a new element called the environment and disclosing many facts that have not even been touched on in traditional world history. Nevertheless, Diamond's effort reaches only halfway to a new world history.

Such an approach to history from the periphery of historical studies as environmental history is extremely effective in re-examining accepted ideas seen in the political/economic/social/cultural histories that have been the center of traditional historical studies and digging up new themes. Because environmental history pays special attention to interactions between people and the environment, however, clustering people on earth into groups calls for prudence. It seems advisable to avoid grouping by nationality (of the nation-state) from the beginning, such as Chinese or Spaniard, because this attaches weight to politics and ethnicity. Simple clustering by so-called cultural spheres, i.e., Europeans, Muslims, and so on, should also be avoided. These groupings are tantamount to a kind of cultural reductionism and they are bound to lead to such simplistic arguments as "Europeans have dealt with the environment in this way." While a bird's eye sketch is indispensable, it will be necessary in this field where the available data is limited to first to accumulate solid individual studies.

[*28] Ibid., 410.

DISCOVERY OF RELATIONSHIPS AND INTERCONNECTEDNESS AMONG GROUPS OF PEOPLE

Exchanges throughout Eurasia

The second method for accomplishing a new world history that surpasses the present world history is to pay attention to commonalities among groups of people and, on that basis, to then describe a history which attaches much value to relationships and interconnectedness among groups of people. One of the greatest problems of the present world history is its inclination to demarcate one group of people from another and follow history by clusters, such as civilization, regional world, and nation-state. It is undeniable that each nation-state or region on earth has its own distinct characteristics. Conventional world history tends to emphasize these characteristics and stress differences among various groups. In contrast, the new world history that I am advocating will continue to recognize these differences but, as I have repeatedly explained, it will pay more attention to the discovery of commonalities among these characteristics. To accomplish this, it will be necessary to effectively use the comparative method. Also, historians are advised to apply a writing style that clearly demonstrates that all regions in the entire world have been interrelated and interconnected with each other in one way or another.

According to the interpretation of world history prevalent nowadays—which, as we've seen, is heavily Euro-centric—advancements of "Europeans" into various regions in the world since the late fifteenth century promoted unification of the world, which had been fragmented previously. This interpretation is based on the belief that a global-scale economic network was organized around Europe through the overseas advancements of "Europeans." According to world-systems theory, which has a high affinity with the Euro-centric historical view, it was around the sixteenth century that a "world economy" was believed to have made its appearance in northwestern Europe. It is beyond doubt that the sixteenth century was a major turning point in the sense that the Americas and Eurasia/Africa became connected through the migration of people in this period. In retrospect, however, one wonders if people in Eurasia and Africa had really lived apart from each other by region or by cultural sphere with no contact among themselves before the fifteenth century.

To be sure, there exist many inventions and discoveries made by people somewhere in the world that did not diffuse to other places for a long time. These include, for instance, elements that are necessities of day-to-day life such as clothes and food, as well as materials and styles of construction. It is hard for these items to travel because people's lifestyles have to respond, to a significant degree, to climate and vegetation, which differ from region to region. It can be said that distinct cultures have flourished all over the world because the most basic elements of the lives of humankind, including clothing, food, and housing, are diverse. In this sense, the world truly is fragmented by cultural sphere. It was only recently, perhaps after the latter half of the twentieth century when humankind became capable of controlling nature to some extent with the help of energy, that people all over the world started wearing t-shirts and jeans and eating sushi and pizza.

But, come to think of it, isn't all of humankind today descended from a female who had lived in eastern Africa some 200,000 years ago? A group of her descendants must have departed Africa to migrate to various places, from Eurasia to Oceania and even the Americas. In this sense, humankind had not been fragmented from the beginning. Jared Diamond stated that, once farming technology was invented at one place in the world, it spread to various places located on the same latitude at considerable speed. Letters that had first begun to be used in several places in the world were diffused not only to their vicinities but also to quite remote areas, where the locals made modifications.

Christianity and Islam, both of which originated in West Asia, spread almost to the entire expanse of the Eurasian continent, while Buddhism, which originated in South Asia, spread everywhere and even reached the remote archipelago of Japan to the east of Eurasia. East Asian inventions such as paper, the compass, and gunpowder reached all the way to the western tip of Eurasia. People from West and Central Asia headed towards the east in great numbers via the so-called Silk Road as well as sea routes. Settlements of these migrants already existed in the cities of Chang'an and Guangzhou by the seventh to ninth centuries. Through these networks, the products of various regions in Eurasia, albeit mainly luxury goods, had been transported to other regions since ancient times.

There are numerous other cases of such Eurasian-wide interactions in the pre-fifteenth-century era. And it is not that the situation drastically changed after the sixteenth century. The only thing that changed was that after the sixteenth century, the people of Western Europe advanced directly into Asian seas via the Cape of Good Hope. While it was undoubtedly an epoch making development for Western Europeans (and, therefore, from the viewpoint of the Euro-centric historical view), it was not a fundamental change from the viewpoint of the region-wide interactions in Eurasia. Whether the world in the past was fragmented by region or not really depends on how we perceive the past.

World History of Goods

That wide-ranging commercial and economic activities have been conducted on earth from ancient times is beyond doubt. For a long time, such luxurious goods as silk, ivory, rare spices, and precious metals remained the main commodities traded. Since around the eighteenth century, however, due to lively trade activities by the northwest Europeans and development of their plantation farming, the volume of trade of such day-to-day commodities (which used to be luxury items themselves) as tea, coffee, sugar, and cotton fabric expanded. Furthermore, various places in the world became specialized in the production of these commodities. By portraying the patterns of production, trade, and consumption of these commodities, one can effectively demonstrate that the activities and lives of peoples in the world are interconnected via these commodities. This method would allow an original, concrete, and easy-to-understand narration of world history. A number of research works based on this method have already been published, including Kawakita Minoru's *Satō no sekaishi* (World history of sugar),[*29] a masterpiece that is often cited as a book representative of this method. Other works have also been published centered around commodities such as coffee, tea, potatoes, and silver.

It should be noted, however, that portrayal of world history based on this method is quite possible without discarding the conventional Euro-centric historical interpretation. For instance, in Kawakita's book, too, the terms "Europe" and "Europeans" are used almost without any premise. Thus, in this book, Europeans prior to the fifteenth century were Christians as a whole, while they were Spaniards and Portuguese during the time of Columbus, and, after the eighteenth century, they came to mean mainly British but, occasionally, French and Americans, too. This is a manifestation of the conventional Euro-centric historical interpretation and description that presuppose the existence of "Europe" as a concept.

While superimposition of production, distribution, and consumption of goods on the conventional world historical interpretation gives the impression of something new and unconventional, this alone would not constitute a new world history, just like Diamond's environmental history book would not. Most books on the history of goods that have been published so far, including not only works in the Japanese language but also those in other languages, are still permeated with this style of historical view.

Japan boasts a few internationally renowned scholars who have published outstanding research works on trade and economy in the Asian region, including Sugihara Kaoru and Hamashita Takeshi, among others. Their works must be highly praised for providing proof of the significance and importance of intra-Asian trade in the nineteenth through twentieth centuries. While their works provide useful data for a new world history, the works themselves, however, have not yet reached the stage of a completed new world history.

[*29] Kawakita Minoru, *Satō no sekaishi* [World history of sugar] (Tokyo: Iwanami Shoten, 1996).

I have come to this conclusion because these books presuppose the presence of Asia as a contraposition to "Europe," in accordance with the conventional framework of world history perception, and detailed analysis of economic activities is limited only to those within this space (i.e., Asia). Thus, the moment the flow of money, goods, and people heading for "Europe" departs toward Europe, they fade from these authors' interest and eyesight. In actuality, "Asia" and "Europe" did not exist separately, nor were economic activities conducted within these two spaces independent of one another. The new world history must refrain from demarcating economic activities in "Europe" and those in "Asia" and, instead, treat and analyze them as an interconnected entity. While tremendous hardships may lie ahead, such as analyzing data and the massive amount of past studies, as well as the need to reinterpret a conventional narrative of "European" history, to name only a few, I would like to see Japanese historians taking the lead in this field because, in my judgment, they are in the best position in the world to do so.

Potential of a History of Maritime World

Recently, the term "maritime world" or "thalassic world" has come to be used often in historical descriptions. The term has been adopted even by high school textbooks in Japan. Ordinarily, a maritime world refers to a space made of a sea in the middle and lands that surround the sea. When history is conceived around land, the sea hardly enters historians' eyesight. But when one conceives a maritime world, the sea itself becomes the center of vision. By putting the sea and surrounding lands together and portraying history with special attention to the movements of people, goods, and information within that space and the interrelations among them, it becomes obvious that a national border, which is a border between two countries whose territories are mostly terrestrial, is not an absolute border. This approach would reveal that people, goods, and information are interlinked with each other and move around dynamically across national borders. Thus, to conceive history in the framework of a maritime world could lead to relativization of the attitude that takes a nation-state and its national border for granted and thus understands the past within that geographical framework. In this sense, a history of the maritime world does certainly have the potential to lead us to a new world history.

The perception of a maritime world was first introduced by French historian Fernand Braudel, in his *La Méditerranée et le Monde Méditerranéen a l'époque de Philippe II* (*The Mediterranean and the Mediterranean World in the Age of Philip II*).[*30] This book puts the Mediterranean in the center and tries to grasp and describe the history of the sea and its surroundings as a whole. Braudel also stresses that, to understand history, one has to be aware of three different flows of time—"geographical time," or the history of relations between people and the environment; "social time," or the history of various groups of people; and "individual time," or the history of events. Braudel stresses the role that geography and the natural environment of the Mediterranean and its surroundings played on the historical development of the region; at the outset of the book, he gives a detailed explanation of this environmental factor as a structure that was long sustained. Braudel's book, which was published in 1949, strongly impacted contemporary historical and academic circles that had taken for granted the grasp and understanding of humankind's past in the framework of the nation-state, such as France and Germany. Subsequent historical studies, too, were greatly influenced by the book.

This method of maritime-centric historical understanding has been subsequently applied to the Indian Ocean, Southeast Asia, and the East and South China Seas, too, producing a number of remarkable outcomes. This method to conceive such geographical spaces as the Atlantic (maritime) world and the Indian Ocean (maritime) world, not to mention the Mediterranean (maritime) world, has also become acceptable to a considerable degree in the Japanese circle of historical studies. For instance, *Iwanami kōza sekai rekishi* (Collection of studies on the history

---

*30 Fernand Braudel, *La Méditerranée et le Monde Méditerranéen a l'époque de Philippe II* [*The Mediterranean and the Mediterranean World in the Age of Philip II*] (Paris: Armand Colin, 1949).

of the world, published by Iwanami Shoten), which greatly influenced the formation of the perception of world history among the Japanese, adopted such frameworks of historical studies as the Indian Ocean world and the Atlantic world in its second series. During a five-year joint research project named Maritime Cross-Cultural Exchange in East Asia and the Formation of Japanese Traditional Culture (led by Kojima Tsuyoshi, then associate professor at the University of Tokyo) that was conducted from 2005 through 2009, an attempt was made to envision a space called the "East Asian maritime world" and to comprehensively grasp its history. As we have seen from these examples, the road to a new world history via the concept of a maritime world has already been paved to a considerable degree.

Weak Point of the Maritime World Concept

The contribution of the maritime world concept notwithstanding, I hold the view that, as a foundation for a new world history, this concept has weak points which we cannot ignore. This concept is liable to bring in a new, geographically closed framework or space to historical studies. The maritime world concept generally refers to a geographical space made of a specific sea, such as the Mediterranean or the Indian Ocean, and the surrounding land. Perception of a maritime world presupposes the existence of common characteristics in that space that demarcate it from other spaces or some kind of interconnectedness among events that occur within that space.

The maritime world is certainly an extremely effective space setting events exploring commonalities and relations among historical incidents that take place in a wider space beyond the boundary of a nation-state. As such, the maritime world concept points to the limit of the nation-state based historical understanding. However, when a term "World A" is used, for example, it presupposes that this world has some kind of common characteristics or coherence that distinguishes itself from other spaces like World B or World C. This is easily understood when one thinks of the Islamic world or "Europe (or European world)" instead of

World A, B, or C. The same situation could take place in the case of the maritime world. As a matter of fact, such authorities in the history of the maritime world as K. N. Chaudhuri and Yajima Hikoichi came up with an Indian Ocean maritime world, a space that has different characteristics from the Mediterranean maritime world, and discussed its history. These two maritime worlds are different, according to them. It is ironic that the concept of a maritime world, which is supposed to criticize historical understanding and description within a closed "nation-state" framework, has ended up creating another, albeit wider, closed framework. I see a type of paradox here.

We must settle this problem in order to accomplish a description of the new world history. When we take another look at the issue, we come to realize that, when we conceive a space centered around a sea, the range of a space that has to be considered as a unit as well as the expansion of land surrounding the sea to be included in the space depends on what characteristics and relationships we use as criteria. And this is a key to the solution of the problem.

For illustration, let us take as an example a space centered around the East China Sea, which is surrounded by the Japanese archipelago, the Korean Peninsula, and mainland China. In the past, junks were often used on this sea. Therefore, the range of a junk's navigation can be used to define a space. Similarly, ranges of trading in this area for such commodities as silk, ginseng, and silver each constitute other spaces. The ranges of the diffusion of Zen Buddhism and Mazu (Chinese goddess of the sea) across the sea are also spaces. One can similarly envision a space where soy sauce is used and a space where chopsticks are used, too. There are countless other factors that can be used to envision a coherent space, including the range of influence of a political entity (the Qing dynasty, the Tokugawa shogunate, etc.) on another overseas political entity; a space where Christianity was banned; and a space where communication is possible by the medium of kanji. When the East China Sea is placed in the center, all of these spaces are spread over the sea, but the boundary of each space varies one by one.

I wonder if a unit made of multiple layers of such diverse virtual spaces (which can be likened to layers used in computer graphics) over a geographical sea can be labeled as a maritime world. The size and expansion of each layer is not uniform. Naturally, the range of a junk's navigation in the eighteenth century (roughly speaking, the East China Sea and the South China Sea), for instance, does not coincide with the space in which Christianity was banned (Japan, Korea, and Qing China). Therefore, the outer boundary of this maritime world remains obscure. Some layers, such as the layer of silver distribution, might well expand endlessly to cover the entire globe. It is also only natural for two or more different maritime worlds with different names to overlap in multiple layers over a specific geographical point. Indeed, this does often happen. For example, the Maluku Islands, the "Spice Islands" producing nutmeg, mace and cloves, are surely to be included in a number of maritime worlds such as the Mediterranean, the Indian Ocean, and South China Sea maritime worlds.

Thus, only by refraining from conceiving a maritime world as a space with a geographical border, could maritime world history be freed from the constraint imposed on conventional historical description as represented by nation-state history, which can be characterized as a diachronic history of incidents in a particular closed space.

Of course, even if this concept of a maritime world were adopted, there would still be those who criticize this method. Their argument can be summarized as follows: "Even if a boundary for each world is not clearly defined, when multiple maritime worlds are envisioned, the histories of each of those maritime worlds would differ. In this sense, a maritime world history is no different from the conventional world history understanding that emphasizes differences." I would respond to this criticism by pointing out that instead of dividing the world into distinct geographical maritime worlds—that is, in a way that a world jigsaw puzzle is completed when several pieces of maritime worlds are assembled—we can think in terms of layers of multiple maritime worlds existing on top of each other. This way of thinking does not make each maritime world a completely separate entity. The potential of a history of the maritime world depends very much on whether those who wish to study and portray the history of each maritime world can envision an outwardly open space instead of a self-contained closed space.

The most important thing is to return the static conventional historical view to the drawing board. We have been too accustomed to the single nation historical view centered around a nation-state for far too long. Of course, seeing as states are real existences, we cannot say that this kind of historical view is unnecessary. But it cannot be an absolute view to be followed unconditionally, either. A perspective of the past that relativizes the nation-state history, instead of a world history that is a mixed bag of nation-state histories, is indispensable when conceiving a new, holistic and integrated world history. From that viewpoint, it will be quite meaningful to set up an experimental ground called a maritime world.

CHAPTER 4

CONCEIVING
A NEW
WORLD HISTORY

FOR CREATION OF A NEW WORLD HISTORY

Fruits of Collaborative Research

The new world history needs no "definitive edition." As long as its description of history makes people realize that there is one world and encourages people to harbor a sense of belonging to the global community, it is a new world history. The world history that we are going to conceive, therefore, does not have to be anything flashy. In fact, it can be something commonsensical. All that is needed is to realize some of the suggestions I made in chapter 3 and increase the number of descriptions suitable to a new world history one by one. As these descriptions catch people's attention, they will become much talked about here and there, inducing more people to read them. Through this process, people's perception of history will change gradually.

At this point, this is the best that I can propose.

Yet I would not presume to end this book with this proposal only. Seeing as I have disparaged the precious research outcomes of my forerunners, it is only fitting that I present my own concrete ideas. In the following pages, I will outline the concept and approach I would take if I were to create a new world history myself. I am the first to admit that such will have to be a skeleton of a very rudimentary plan. There still remain numerous points to be researched and clarified in order to make my outline more persuasive and appealing.

Ordinarily, a scholar would not disclose his scheme while it is still in the planning stages—like a pre-performance rehearsal piece, so to speak. If allowed to do so, I, too, would wish to gestate my plan a little longer. But to get people thinking about a new world history as promptly as possible, I have decided to share with readers what is far from a complete plan. It is my wish that this premature disclosure of my plan will invigorate discussions on a new world history, generate interest by as many people as possible in history—world history, in particular—and encourage people to think about their awareness of themselves as global citizens.

To tackle such a gigantic issue as how to grasp world history, it is better to team up with like-minded individuals so that we can learn from each other's wisdom rather than to work alone. With that in mind, since 2009, I have conducted joint research under the title of "Eurasia in the Modern Period: Towards a New World History" with the help of the Grants-in-Aid for Scientific Research program of the Japan Society for the Promotion of Science. For details on this project, readers are encouraged to visit <http://haneda.ioc.u-tokyo.ac.jp/english/eurasia/>. I have already benefitted a lot from discussions with my highly motivated colleagues when formulating the two methods that I discussed in chapter 3—the elimination of centricity and the discovery of mutual relationship—as well as my private plan that I am about to share with readers. Needless to say, final responsibility falls solely on me, and I wish to note here that my private plan is also an interim report of collaborative works with my colleagues.

In the following section, I intend to first present my thoughts on what language should be employed to describe world history and on the multiplicity of world histories. Discussion of a more concrete concept for the new world history will follow.

Language to Be Employed to Describe World History

In what language should the world history of the global community be written? This inevitable question for a narrator of world history is indeed a prickly one. Recently, I have come to have some conviction about this issue—and that is, it does not matter what language is employed as long as people all over the world can sense that "This is our own world history." Not too many Japanese are proficient in writing in English. The number of Japanese who can read world history written in English and perfectly comprehend its contents is also limited. Therefore, I believe it would be advisable for Japanese historians to formulate their concept of a new world history in the Japanese language and publish the outcome in the same language. Similarly, there also should be new world histories written in, say, Chinese and Arabic.

It should be noted, however, that it would be immensely problematic if a number of world histories were written in multiple languages, sometimes with totally different contents, without knowledge of each other's contents. Even when world history is written in diverse languages, efforts should be made to encourage each writer to know the contents of other world histories and to align with those contents and basic stances as much as possible. To that end, translations of world histories will be indispensable for historians all over the world to understand and refer to world histories written in foreign languages. And it is this translation that causes a problem.

While all the languages in the world have a number of commonalities with each other in terms of vocabulary and expressions, each one of them has its own distinct system of meanings and values. And the situation is no different for English, which has become the de facto lingua franca in today's world. The English language has vocabulary and structure that make it easy for its native speakers to express their own worldview and values. For this reason, it often happens that, when sentences in the Japanese language, with its own distinct vocabulary and structure, are made to fit the context and the system of meanings and values of English language, the original meaning is sometimes distorted or made incomprehensible. It is not an easy task to replace a text written in the Japanese language with its English translation without changing meanings.

Take, for instance, this word "world history" that we have been talking about. The position that this particular word occupies in the system of meanings and values is subtly different from one language to another. While the word "world history," or *sekaishi*, is directly linked to high school curricula and university entrance examinations and, as such, it produces certain specific images in people's minds in Japan, world history is a highly peculiar concept in France, where extra explanations are called for to ensure accurate understanding. In the English language, both "world history" and "global history" are used, neither one of which fits perfectly with the meaning of the term *sekaishi* in the Japanese language.

Let us take another example. The Japanese word *kokka* is used almost throughout the entire span of Japanese history and Chinese history, and it can be said that the word represents an almost self-evident concept for the Japanese and the Chinese. This term is ordinarily translated as state, nation, or country in the English language. But, depending on the context, such words as kingdom, empire, or dynasty are also used to express *kokka*. In some instances, government might be a more appropriate translation. Depending on which of the above possibilities is chosen, the content of the sentence can vary significantly when it is translated to English. Some may criticize that the term *kokka* is not sufficiently differentiated as a concept. Seen from another angle, however, it may be said that the English language does not have a word or concept that can fully express the meaning of *kokka*.

In contrast to the case of *kokka*, some words in English can be translated into several different Japanese words. Whereas "I" is the only first-person singular pronoun used in English, the Japanese language has a number of first-person pronouns from which to choose according to the situation. Thus, it often happens that one-to-one correspondence cannot be found between an English word and a Japanese word. It is not proper to think that the vocabulary or the expressiveness of one language is superior or inferior to another. It is indeed needless to say, that the English and Japanese languages differ significantly in their systems of meanings and values as well as expressions that are linked to the respective systems.

To Hone the English Language

It is no use resorting to a "so-what attitude," claiming it is impossible to translate a world history in one language to a different language because each language has its own distinct system of values and meanings. According to this view, world history should be written in the language of each country, paying no heed to world history in other languages. I am of the view, however, that repeated attempts should be made to realize translations that are mutually comprehensible. Japanese scholars who are proficient in the English language may advocate that a world history should be written in English from the start, because

English is the de facto lingua franca. I disagree with this argument. For a Japanese to write a world history in English from the start is tantamount to accepting the current system of meanings and values of the English language and arguing within that framework. The English language today is still a language of its native speakers; it has not attained the level of a genuine lingua franca yet. Thus, we in Japan will have to translate meanings and values in the Japanese language into English as accurately as possible. By doing so, we will facilitate the evolution of the English language, so to speak.

This may sound hopelessly tedious, but we seem to have no other choice than to first explain *in English* the structure of the Japanese language and the meaning of terminologies and concepts as well as their configurations within this structure (in other words, the structure of the Japanese language as a whole) in a comprehensive manner, after which we can try to charge individual English words with new meanings or create new English words.

The above abstractive explanation may defy easy comprehension. Let me take up a concrete example. The Japanese words *shūkyō* and *sezoku* came into use during the Meiji era after being charged with the meanings of "religion" and "secular," respectively. Buried behind these two English words were the situation of Christendom at the time and an interpretation of the history that had brought about the situation. In contrast, these two words pay no heed to situations in Japan around the same time. The situation in Japan and the history that had brought about this situation must have been considerably different from that of Christendom. Nevertheless, the concepts of religion and secular were adopted by the Japanese language in the form of *shūkyō* and *sezoku*, and these words subsequently came to be configured and integrated in the system of values and meanings of the Japanese language. Today, these two Japanese words are often used when narrating pre-Meiji history—a time when these concepts must have been absent. Naturally, there should be a subtle difference between the meanings of the original English words as used in the system of the English language and the two Japanese words as used in the system of the Japanese language.

What I am proposing is to explain in English the meaning of the words *shūkyō* and *sezoku* and subsequently to charge the English words "religion" and "secular" with these meanings—or, when that is not possible, to create new English words that correspond to these meanings. If that, too, turns out to be too difficult, we must at least make people for whom English is their mother/native tongue understand that the meaning of the words *shūkyō* and *sezoku*, as used when discussing the past of the Japanese archipelago, are not equivalent to the meaning of the words "religion" and "secular" in contemporary English language. In order to promote mutual understanding between the two language systems, the above procedure must be patiently continued for all the major concepts and terminologies.

Of course, this problem is not confined to the relationship between the Japanese and English languages. Similar efforts should be made between English and such non-European languages as Chinese and Arabic as well as between English and other European languages, including French and German. By continuing these efforts, the English language will be enriched in terms of expressiveness and vocabulary, and thus upgraded to a genuine lingua franca.

Asymmetrical Paradox

Behind my argument for the tempering of the English language is the existence of an interesting paradox in the world language situation. While systems of meanings and values of the European languages, including English, may differ from each other to significant degrees, particularly in the details, as a whole the systems can be labeled "modern Western knowledge." Anthropologist Talal Asad regards this modern Western knowledge as a kind of power. For instance, when the relationship between politics and religion in today's Saudi Arabia, which belongs to a different system of language and knowledge, is analyzed through the lens of the ideas and understanding of modern Western knowledge, the latter has the power to condemn the Saudi situation as unmodern.

In the late nineteenth century through to the first half of the twentieth century, it was considered that modern Western knowledge was universal intelligence for humankind and as such should be learned and obtained by every human being. It is almost a common understanding in today's academic circles, however, that modern Western knowledge was formed against the backdrop of the worldview of a specific group of people who believed themselves to belong to a certain specific space (i.e., "Europe" as a concept, or the West) and that, as such, it has certain limitations. In this sense, Asad's assertion, which may surprise many who are exposed to it for the first time, is actually a very legitimate, commonsensical argument.

In my judgment, today's English language still remains within the confines of this modern Western knowledge in terms of its expressions, vocabulary, and manners of thinking. English is, therefore, still a language of people who speak it as a mother tongue. In contrast, speakers of many of the non-European languages, including Japanese, had understood and incorporated the modern Western knowledge into their own languages since the nineteenth century and, on that basis, constructed their own systems of meanings and values. Furthermore, these non-European peoples have continuously and steadily made efforts to understand their societies and histories from angles that are different from the "European" viewpoint. Thus, once the authority and universality of modern Western knowledge are called into question, thus putting all the language systems on earth on a par, would it not be possible, quite ironically, that non-European languages are found to be endowed with richer and more versatile semantic contents than European languages?

And this is the reason, I argue, that as much concrete information on the systems of meanings and values of non-European languages as possible should be transplanted into the English language, upon which efforts should be made to construct a new system of values and meanings. Seeing as the systems of values and meanings of the two sides have not been identical from the beginning, this will be a very difficult task. Recalling that the modern Western knowledge had once transformed the non-European societies and their systems of meanings and values, however, it should not be an impossible task. It is only after the English language fully incorporates non-European information narrated in respective contexts and ceases to narrate information in a distinctively "European" or "Western" context that it can become a genuine lingua franca.

What I propose here is, of course, an ideal theory. It should not be possible to enable the English language to communicate expressions and meanings of all the languages on earth so easily. And, if the English language becomes bloated with too many expressions and meanings, it may become difficult to use. If the English language should ever be transformed into such an omnipotent language, the Japanese language may be destined to perish. But even with such a risk, I am convinced that we must try to transmit messages in the English language. English today has become an influential language not only in the world of business but also in academic circles. Yet it is still permeated with a distinctively modern Western worldview. Conscientious scholars must point out each and every example of such a worldview and help temper the English language to a genuine lingua franca.

Multiple New World Histories

Let me discuss another important problem associated with a new world history aside from the problem of language. It has to do with whether there should be an ultimate new world history or, to put it another way, whether there should be only one new world history. I for one do not think that there is only one ultimate new world history. What is important in conceiving a new world history is what attitude we take when looking back on the past. The stance that "there is one world" is the premise for describing a new world history. As long as this stance is shared, it will be a new world history no matter what approach is taken or in which language it is written.

Even the interpretation and portrayal of Japanese history has been subject to a number of contending views. One might go so far as to say that the only commonality among them is the framework of Japan and the Japanese as their premise. If such is true about the history of only one nation-state, Japan, then it would be utterly impossible to conceive only one "ultimate" world history. The first step to be taken is to try a variety of new approaches to conceive and portray a world history. We should feel rewarded if and when there emerges a common theme, or *basso continuo* if you will, penetrating these numerous new approaches and portraits stacked up one on another. And this common theme will be the message that "there is one world."

As discussed in the preceding chapter, the present world history is understood differently in each country. Yet a tacit premise that attaches weight to the Euro-centric historical view and the history of each country has been running like an undercurrent throughout these different understandings. From this angle, we should probably say that there already is a common world history in the present world. In this case, though, *basso continuo* is the importance attached to the Euro-centric historical view and separate national histories. In the new world history that I am proposing, the basic premise should be the notion that "there is one world." As long as this message comes through, there can be a variety of world history portrayals. The new world history can be likened to a symphony. Violins, violas, trumpets, cymbals, and many other instruments play different tunes, but together they form a beautiful piece of music.

Conversely, I am not of the view that the past of the world can be presented in a unified manner in accordance with certain theories. I doubt, therefore, that a single world history that satisfies all can be portrayed. The Marxist history has shown an inclination toward such a unified world history, and there are some who wish to pursue its line further to construct new theories and laws. While I have nothing against this, I personally would like to pursue an effort toward the opposite direction. While "there is one world" indeed, the personalities, circumstances, and ways of thinking of its dwellers are diverse. Therefore, I believe it is only natural that there be diverse understandings and descriptions of world history. As long as we are standing on the same earth, there is no need for everyone to be facing in the same direction. Thus, there should be multiple descriptions of world history.

As far as Japan is concerned, it is desirable that explanations of the past that convey the message "there is one world" be incorporated in high school textbooks so that people can obtain a worldview through history classes that is suitable to the present. Looking back at the steps that the curriculum guideline of the Ministry of Education, Science, Sports and Culture (MEXT) has taken so far, however, it does not seem easy to accomplish this. This is because it will be only after historians' common sense changes, leading to changes in their research results, which are reflected in the contents of the curriculum guideline, that new textbooks based on a new perception of world history will actually be written and published.

Given all the difficulties, it would not be surprising if it takes a long time to get explanations of the past which convey the message "there is one world" incorporated into high school textbooks. However, we cannot afford to waste too much time. We should release historical interpretations and descriptions toned by the new world history—even portions of them if necessary—as soon as possible. Elements that are necessary for compiling a textbook will be picked up from them, organized, and made into textbooks of the new world history. As long as *basso continuo* is shared, it is, in fact, better for the contents of these textbooks to be diverse. While today's high school textbooks in Japan are all similar in terms of content, I believe textbooks of the new world history should be more diverse. The content of what is described should differ significantly, depending on the angle from which one is trying to understand the past and what to emphasize when describing the past. If the curriculum guideline is still called for after textbooks of the new world history are compiled, its function should be confined to regulating the basic view on world history. All the rest should be left to individual textbooks and their authors.

THREE METHODS

Direction to Be Taken

Finally, we have reached the point of discussing the actual concept of the new world history. When conceiving a new world history, the first choice one has to make is whether to portray the history of the earth or the history of humankind. If one attaches weight to the viewpoint of environmental history, it would be essential to organize and present the history of the earth before that of humankind. Because the earth has been the place where humankind has lived throughout all time, it is a matter of course to discuss first how this living venue evolved and what condition it is in. The past of the entire ecological system on earth, including animals and vegetation, should also be studied. Furthermore, because humankind is, so to speak, a product of stardust of the universe, the 13.7 billion-year history of the universe should also be addressed. Honestly speaking, however, these mega histories are beyond my capacity at this point. Taking into consideration that humankind's history is just a blink of an eye compared to the histories of the earth or the universe and understanding that the demarcation of humankind from animals and vegetation is for convenience sake, I would like to concentrate here on portraying the history of humankind.

The next issue is the overall picture. As discussed earlier, as long as an author's position that he/she is writing a portion of the overall world history is clearly stated, what he/she produces would be a new world history even when he/she writes only about a certain era or a certain aspect of world history. Therefore, there can be a variety of new world histories. In order to clarify the difference between conventional world history and the new world history, I intend here to focus on drawing the overall picture of world history.

As I have repeatedly argued so far, the standard world history in Japan has been constructed around the history of "Europe" as its center. "Europe" first made its appearance in world history as one of the pre-modern civilizations or regional worlds, and it became the central player after the sixteenth century. In world history from the sixteenth century until the twentieth century, it is customary to divide the world into "Europe" and "non-Europe" and to describe the two histories separately in chronological order within their respective frameworks. In a nutshell, it is described that "Europe" succeeded in developing itself on its own within its own framework and thus created modernity, while "non-Europe," including Japan, received the impact of modernity through advancement of Europe and the West, with which it was inevitably forced to cope.

This kind of worldview and historical perception is unsuited to the present. Let me repeat myself once again. The worldview that is needed today is that which declares that "there is one world." And today's historical perception must correspond to this worldview. We must mend our conventional attitude of understanding world history by demarcating "Europe" and "non-Europe" and develop methods to understand and describe the history of the world as one unit. It can even be said that the success of a new world history depends on how much we can refrain from perceiving "Europe" and its history as special.

The new world history is not to be conceived only to abolish demarcation between "Europe" and "non-Europe." It should also narrate how the values that are cherished in today's world have been created and present the future prospects of human society. In his book *Senryaku gaikō genron* (Principles of strategic diplomacy),[*31] Kanehara Nobukatsu, a leading Japanese diplomat, enumerated the following five values as being important for people to uphold in today's world:

1. Rule of law (Any authority is under rule of law in the broad sense of the term.)
2. Man's dignity (Any person must be valued.)
3. Democratic institutions
4. Renunciation of violence between states (Pursuit of peace)
5. Labor and free market (Proper compensation and free exchanges)

---

*31 Kanehara Nobukatsu, *Senryaku gaikō genron* [Principles of strategic diplomacy] (Tokyo: Nippon Keizai Shimbun Shuppansha, 2011).

I find that Kanehara's arguments have a point, and readers are urged to read this stimulating book for details.

The present world history claims that all of the above values were created by "Europe" and stresses the values differences with "non-Europe." But this is the view of "Europeans." As Kanehara stresses in his book, when one looks back at the past of various regions of the world, particularly that of Japan and China, without any prejudgment, it becomes clear that concepts very similar to the above five values were discussed and attempts were made to realize them in the "non-European" world—but they simply may have been termed differently. In the new world history, efforts should be made to proactively introduce these cases and narrate how humankind has pursued these values from past to present.

Three Methods

What options, then, are there for portraying a new world history? In the first place, we must rid ourselves of the Euro-centric historical view above all else. And in order to accomplish this, it would be basic to eliminate any centricity from the description of history and to explain relationships and the inter-connectedness among peoples all over the world. Keeping these two things in mind, I would like to propose the following three methods.

1. **MAKE A SKETCH OF THE WORLD**

    We should make a sketch of the world by lining up groups of people from all over the world and from one point in time to compare their respective characteristics, simplify these characteristics to abstractive models to help identify differences and commonalities among them, and, thus, grasp the entire picture. Through this method, which does not posit any particular region in the center, it will be revealed that all the European countries did not share the same characteristics and that world history cannot be explained by a simplistic dichotomy between "Europe" and "non-Europe."

2. STOP DWELLING ON DIACHRONIC HISTORY

Using the method just described, we should produce several sketches of the world for different ages and compare them with the overall picture of today's world and its characteristics. It is important here to refrain from ordering these sketches according to chronological order and connecting them to the present by finding continuous or linear relations among them. It is important to compare each of these sketches with the present separately. This way, we should be able to block the conventional and characteristic "European history," in which concept and reality are intermingled, from interfering chronologically with the new world history.

3. BE MINDFUL OF HORIZONTAL CONNECTIONS IN HISTORY

We should discuss in a persuasive way that people the world over have been intimately connected with each other via goods and information and thus mutually influenced. By doing so, people should realize that human beings have been connected and have interacted horizontally and that "Europe" alone has not existed and moved around singlehandedly.

In the following pages, I intend to explain these three methods in more detail. It should be noted at the outset that I will mainly discuss the portrayal of world history up to the first half of the nineteenth century, when "Europe" as a concept was established. Once world history down to this period is thoroughly reviewed, interpretation of subsequent developments in history should automatically change. Available space as well as my limited present capacity do not allow me to sufficiently discuss the interpretation of world history after the latter half of the nineteenth century. And it is my wish to return to this issue some other time.

MAKE A SKETCH OF THE WORLD

Exploring Commonalities and Differences

When we make a sketch of the world, we need to decide the basic unit. I suggest that the basic unit should be a group of people. There are countless criteria for grouping people, including blood relationship, language, regional bond, religion, profession, kin-tract, political power, social class, and culture, to name a few. I choose a group of people equipped with a political system that enables them to establish and maintain social order as the unit for basic observation and description. Such a group may be termed a "societal constituent group." By adopting this unit, we will be able to narrate how numbers one through four of the above five important values for people to uphold in today's world have been treated in various places on earth.

I have a reason to deliberately use the roundabout expression of a "group of people" as the basic unit for comparison instead of a country or a state. When such a unit as a country or a state is used, the diverse characteristics of groups of people are liable to be disregarded, leading to a misunderstanding that a country or a state is an unchanging presence which has existed all over the world continuously from past to present. Humankind must live in groups, and people have organized groups with a variety of social orders and political systems at various times and in various places. We should not forget that such a group configuration as a country or a state is also a historical presence. The terms "country" and "state" can also connote a more impersonal organization rather than a group of people. Even when I use a group as a unit, I wish to attempt to render historical descriptions that allow readers to clearly depict how people lived and behaved in the group.

When a comparative method is applied to narrate world history, the first task is to pick up groups of people created at one point in history one by one so as to discuss and give commentary on the social order of each group and the political mechanism that ensured that order in each group, as well as each group's characteristic culture. The next step is to discuss the characteristics of these groups of people thus picked up and the commonalities across groups, as well as the mutual influences among the groups. Particularly for the pre-nineteenth-century world, we should give careful attention to the fact groups of people were much more diversified and one person more often than not belonged to more than one group, each of which was characterized by one form of social order and political system, when we explain characteristics of groups of people, referring to concrete examples.

For instance, while the Sogdians who resided in the city of Chang'an in the eighth century were under the rule of the Tang dynasty, they also maintained strong ties with their kinsfolk dwelling in Sogdiana (present-day Uzbekistan) in the west, outside the Tang territory. Catholic bishops in seventeenth-century France were leaders of Catholic believers under the spiritual guidance of the pope, but at the same time, they were also de facto assigned to their posts by the French king. Around the same time, coppersmiths in cities on the Iranian Plateau were simultaneously members of the craft guild, local leaders, and subjects of the kings of the Safavid dynasty of the time.

While Sogdian kinsfolk, Catholic believers, and craft guilds may not necessarily be classified as political powers, they all maintained some kind of intragroup order as well as a certain degree of self-governing capabilities. Additionally, the activities of pre-modern diasporas, including massive numbers of Chinese immigrants to Southeast Asia, Jews who played active roles in various regions in Eurasia, and Armenian and Sogdian diasporas, were also an important element which deserves attention in the new world history.

In the new world history, attention is paid to these elements that transcend national boundaries in order to highlight the historicity of sovereign states/nation-states and the structure of the contemporary world, which represents the aggregate of these states. When it is recognized that territory and national sovereignty are inseparable and when the historicity of the contemporary sovereign nation-state system, which has been in a constant state of territorial disputes since all the land territories of the world were divided by states, is understood, good wisdom may emerge to settle unproductive interstate confrontations over territories.

Modeling Groups of People

Concrete questions to be asked for the sake of comparison include the following: How, in diverse regions on earth, have groups of people been composed (basic units and linkage among groups) and how has the social order in these groups been maintained? Have the social roles of men and women differed? If yes, then what kind of differences were there? How has political power engaged in the maintenance of social order? How has the legitimacy of political power been guaranteed? Has there been some relationship between religion and social order? All of these are related to the first through third of the five important values (i.e., the rule of law, human dignity, and democratic institutions).

In the case of a great political power, social structure and its maintenance, as well as the method of government (more concretely, social status, judiciary and administration, tax collection mechanism, etc.), should have differed from region to region, even under the rule of the same regime. This is one point that requires extra attention when dealing with the questions just raised.

Also, the following question, which is concerned about the fourth value (i.e., the pursuit of peace), should be kept in mind: How have peaceful relations between one group of people and another been constructed and maintained? When has an armed conflict erupted between the two? What was the relationship like between a group of people and land/territory?

These questions are rather traditional and more general questions in the realm of historical studies, and answers have already been found to a considerable degree within the framework of national or regional histories. What we need to do is to process these answers confined to the national/regional history contexts into models to enable mutual comparisons and line them up horizontally.

Modeling is a process of extracting elements that appear to

characterize the social order and political system of a certain group of people, paying little heed to case-specific or exceptional features of past incidents, and presenting them clearly in the form of models that allow mutual comparison.

Let me give you an illustration. Imagine a deep forest. Inside the forest are all kinds of trees, each one of which has a different shape. Every tree is distinctive. And yet, those trees can be clustered into groups by species like cedar, oak, camphor, beech, and chinquapin. And when these trees, underbrush, and other vegetation are put together, they form a forest with a distinctive atmosphere.

Human communities on earth are likened to this deep forest. A group of people is an individual tree and, put together, they form a forest. While trees look different from each other and there appears to be no order among them, they can be sorted into clusters by species. Trees have characteristics that are common to a certain group, such as color and shape of leaves and trunks, shape of flowers and fruits, and timing of defoliation, to name a few. When we sort out trees into groups, we almost unconsciously conduct modeling of a tree, because we find the characteristics of a tree and judge which other trees share them and which others do not. Sometimes, one forest is compared with another forest as a next step and it is then sorted out to a coniferous forest, a broad-leaved forest, or some other kind of forest; through this sorting process, a forest as a whole is made into a model.

We can apply basically the same process to groups of people. Groups of people can be made into models to highlight their major characteristics and compare thus-produced models with characteristics of other groups of people in order to identify commonalities and differences. When a sketch of an era is thus made, it can also be made into a model to be compared with a sketch of another era.

Making a Sketch

Let me introduce a concrete example here. Taking the period of the latter half of the seventeenth century, modeling could be attempted in order to address the aforementioned common questions for the following groups of people and line them up on a same plane: the Tokugawa shogunate under Tokugawa Tsunayoshi; the Kingdom of Joseon (Korea) under King Sukjong; the Qing Empire under the Kangxi Emperor; the Dzungar Khanate under Galdan Boshugtu Khan; the Ayutthaya Kingdom under King Narai; the Mughal Empire under Emperor Aurangzeb; the Safavid Empire during the Soleymān era; the Ottoman Empire under Mehmed IV; the Russian Empire under Peter the Great; the Holy Roman Empire under Leopold I; the Republic of the Seven United Netherlands; France under Louis XIV; England immediately after the Glorious Revolution; Spain under Carlos II; groups of diaspora-like people scattered around Eurasia, including Armenians, Jews, and Chinese; colonies in the Americas and the societies of their aboriginal peoples; and groups of people in those regions believed to have no powerful political authority, including regions in Africa and Oceania. By modeling these groups of people, the differences and commonalities among them become apparent, revealing to us characteristic features of human communities in the entire world during this period.

The outcomes of this attempt should be immensely different from the world history understandings found in today's high school textbooks. Today's textbooks describe the histories of European countries country by country, while explanation is given on the establishment of the sovereign state system, which was a common international order in Europe of the time. Since these country-by-country descriptions are independent of each other and are centered around historical events and historical terms in each country, they make cross-country comparison for certain pivotal points impossible. For instance, it is utterly impossible to examine such a basic point as what were the commonalities and differences among the Dutch Republic, the English constitutional monarchy, absolute monarchism in France, and imperialism in the Austrian Empire/Holy Roman Empire. No explanation is given, either, why all of these countries were regarded as sovereign states while non-European countries were not.

In West Asia, South Asia, and East Asia, large-scale dynastic countries (which are also oftentimes called empires) lined up around the same period, including the Ottoman dynasty, the Safavid dynasty, the Mughal dynasty, the Qing dynasty, and Japan, from west to east. Present-day textbooks only present individual characteristics of the political system and social order in each of these dynasties separately; no comparison is made among them or with European countries in the west.

One of the reasons that descriptions in today's textbooks are so much broken into pieces by country is because conventional historical studies have used country or region as the main framework for analysis and synthesis and interpreted historical events solely in the chronological sequences of that particular country/region along the context of historical documents which themselves are recorded in that particular country/region. For instance, the shogunate system in Japan has been interpreted in the context of Japanese history, and its characteristics have been discussed mainly in comparison with the political systems of the preceding and following eras in Japan.

Similarly, the absolute monarchism in France has been interpreted and understood in the context of French history. Political authorities in various countries/regions have been called by diverse names, including dynasties, kingdoms, empires, and Khanate. Most of these names, however, are what they were customarily referred to in the historical descriptions of their respective regions rather than the results of rigorous sorting and grouping based on examination of the political systems of human communities throughout world history.

In the new world history, this kind of country-specific historical understanding as well as any dichotomous understanding—e.g., "Europe" vs. "non-Europe"—would be completely eliminated. The new world history would lay out and examine and compare all the groups of people in the world on the same table from the same angle, and discuss their commonalities and differences. In the actual description, the social order and political systems of characteristic groups of people all over the world would be expounded on one by one, taking into consideration comparisons with other groups of people. During this process, special attention would be paid to how the aforementioned five important values are treated in each group. Subsequently, systematic classification of human communities would be attempted to clarify how groups of people with common characteristics have been distributed throughout the world and how they have been interrelated, upon which a sketch would be drawn that can present a bird's eye view of the entire picture. Done correctly, this sketch should become a complicated illustration that cannot be explained by the world history perception based on a simplistic demarcation between "Europe" and "non-Europe."

Needless to say, it would be impossible to carry out this task alone. It would be only when experts of various regional histories get together to provide reliable data that have been acquired through observations from as similar angles as possible and conduct joint discussions among them that a more precise and persuasive prospect can be obtained. While it is constantly pointed out that originality is the most important thing in research, this particular task should be conducted jointly by a group of researchers who share the same awareness of the problem and use the same method as much as possible. It is also advisable for this group to actively utilize secondary materials, including the findings of other researchers.

PAYING LITTLE HEED TO DIACHRONIC SEQUENCE IN HISTORY

Several Sketches

Let us suppose that we have succeeded in drawing a sketch with a bird's eye view of the entire world at one point in the past by horizontally lining up models of social order and political systems in various groups of people and comparing them. According to the conventional understanding of world history, it becomes an important issue how each of the groups of people on the sketch or the sketch as a whole subsequently evolves. Historians would fervently argue, for instance, about how the political regime of England changed from the seventeenth to eighteenth centuries and what were the causes of changes, or about whether there was a change in social order under the Qing dynasty. Their utmost concern would be to clarify the transition of their research targets along a chronological sequence.

I like to say that the world history that I propose to conceive here, however, would deliberately not pay too much heed to these interpretations along diachronic sequences. Instead, I propose that all the efforts should be devoted to drawing a sketch of the world at one point in the past through comprehensive comparisons among various groups of people. When a sketch of a time in the past is completed, we should move on to a sketch of another arbitrary point in the past, unrelated to the previously completed sketch. We should concentrate on drawing a picture of the entire world at a point in the past, paying special attention to its contrast to the contemporary world but no heed to connections with periods preceding it or following it. As a matter of fact, this method is already adopted, at least partially, by history textbooks in France, as we discussed in chapter 2.

The length of time to be covered by one sketch will probably be about 100 years up to the fifteenth century. It could be ten years or fifty years, but it seems rather challenging to model groups of people in various places in the world every ten years or so in the pre-fifteenth-century period. Yet 300 years or 500 years would be too long. Therefore, 100 years seems to be an appropriate length of time for one sketch to cover.

As this work gets closer to the present time, the amount of information available will increase, and even minor events and their evolutions come within historians' field of vision. Naturally, it becomes difficult to turn the findings into a model simply by leaving out minor details. For these periods, perhaps it is necessary to make a sketch for a shorter period of time than 100 years. That would be fine as long as each sketch can be discussed individually in relation with today's world.

Some may criticize that these sketches are by no means a world history. In response, I suggest that we should line up all the sketches in chronological order and then stack them up. By doing so, we can detect differences among sketches of the world in different times. One important thing is to refrain from the habit of understanding these sketches by simply lining them up chronologically. As I will discuss in the following pages, I believe we should remain cautious when describing a diachronic history of time and space called the "world," for the time being.

This method of stacking several sketches has one big advantage. It can explicitly reveal that the scale of human communities and the geographical expansion of people's life range differed from one period to another. Unlike the conventional world history, there is not necessarily a need to believe that certain specific groups of people have persisted over a long period. It is appropriate, in this method, to consider that characteristic groups of people existed in various places in each period. This way, we should be able to avoid an essentialist historical understanding that a civilization A, a country B, or a culture C has existed unchanged since olden days.

For example, in a region of the world where a large-scale group of people M had previously existed in the last century BCE/CE, four groups of people P, Q, R, and S with different characteristics emerged in the tenth century. And let us suppose that the sum of the geographical spaces connected to these four groups does not exactly match the space in which the group M had once dwelled and acted. In the conventional world history, in which it is customary to describe history according to chronological sequence, how to relate these groups of people in two different time periods is an important point of contention. Readers only have to recall the descriptions of present Chinese history to understand this problem. In the new world history, this hardly becomes an issue because it only applies a bird's eye view to the world of, say, the last century BCE and the tenth century to grasp the entire picture. There is no need to discuss, for instance, if the Han and Tang dynasties are the same China or not.

It would be the same for "Europe," which is a point of interest, too. The world sketch of the sixteenth century and that of the eighteenth century, naturally, must be quite different. There is no need to inquire, for instance, which group of people in the sixteenth century constituted

"Europe" and what happened to this group in the eighteenth century. The important thing is to use world sketches of different times to understand the characteristics and structure of the contemporary world and vice versa. In this case, "Europe" is a concept or an idea and it is not the social order or political system per se of an actual group of people. This would be understood clearly once one is freed from a chronological understanding of world history.

Comparison with the Present Time

Sketches of the world in the past are drawn to compare them with today's world. It is expected that, by gazing at the past world and knowing its conditions, we will be able to understand the characteristics of the contemporary world more accurately. Needless to say, the very benefit of learning history is that it lets us understand the present time.

What I am proposing here is that we should draw sketches of our past, paying special attention to order in groups of people and the political systems that maintained that order. I believe that, by giving a little twist to the way we describe and explain the past, people's view on the contemporary world would be changed, even when we use the same materials that are used in the present world history. When drawing sketches, we should pay special attention to the five aforementioned values. We should also attempt to provide descriptions that allow for an easy understanding of how these five values were treated in various places in the world in the past. From different sketches of the past, one would be able to extract a lot of different, useful information. It would be ideal if the information acquired helped us recognize the characteristics of today's world that attach weight to these values, as well as the importance of establishing these values.

When one takes a closer look at the world at one point in the past, it should be recognized that one group of people and another group of people were not necessarily aware of the boundaries of their respective territories. There were eras and regions, like Southeast Asia, in which wars erupted not over territories but over people. From these cases, it should be understood that the notion that all the land areas on earth are territories of one sovereign country or another is by no means a constant throughout history. It should also be understood that territorial disputes between sovereign nations are phenomena characteristic of modern and contemporary times. It is meaningless to argue whose territories the Takeshima and Senkaku islands had originally been.

Examination of the sketches of the world in different times would also confirm that the notion that all statistics, including those on production and trade, should be calculated and aggregated on a country basis and then used to measure country by country the national power of each, thus pleasing or saddening the country, is a particularly contemporary phenomenon. In the Indian Ocean maritime world in the sixteenth century, for instance, "country" hardly ever regulated the trade activities of merchants, and it did not matter at all from which "state" those merchants hailed. I suspect the merchants had no idea that they were working for a particular "state" at all, either. The concept of "free trade" itself is a particularly modern-contemporary invention. And this capacity to spotlight the present time and clarify its characteristics in comparison with the past is the usefulness inherent in history.

At the same time, it is also important to view the past from the perspective of the present and spotlight aspects of the past that have been forgotten. We should make conscious efforts to excavate, based on contemporary concerns, aspects of the past that have not necessarily received special attention previously—including, for example, relations between human beings and the environment or, more concretely, their technology for developing natural resources and their use of such resources.

What is considered important in today's world is different from person to person. It would be marvelous if each of us can extract useful information from the past in our own way and, by so doing, disclose new aspects of the past by applying contemporary concerns to days gone by. In any event, the important thing is to facilitate a dialogue between the present and the past. We should constantly keep this basic stance in mind.

Banishment of Diachronic History

In this book, I have often referred to the term "diachronic history" without any further explanation. At this point, let me spare a few pages to elaborate on this term.

Things transform as time goes on. It is common to describe history by tracing the process of this transformation and giving its reasons and consequences as explanations. This is how we interpret day-to-day experiences of ours. It is what I call understanding the past as diachronic history. While it may appear to be a very natural way to perceive the past, it is actually a unique historical view based on the concept that time irreversibly and linearly flows from the past to the future. In the past, some subscribed to a historical view based on cyclical time and repetitive time; not all the people in the world had the chronological historical view.

The Japanese, when trying to understand the past, are particularly fond of historical descriptions projected through the lens of diachronic history. It has been customary for the history of Japan as a state to be described from the past to the present in chronological sequence, and this might be one of the reasons behind the Japanese preference. It should be noted that this historical understanding of Japan did not begin in the Meiji era with the importation of German historiographical methodology. Evidence that the Japanese have long had this historical understanding includes the *Jinnō shōtōki* (Chronicles of the authentic lineages of the divine emperors) of the Northern and Southern Courts period in the fourteenth century, which was an attempt at capturing Japanese history chronologically against the backdrop of the permanence of the emperor's family; the Kokugaku, a school of Japanese philology and philosophy; and the *Dai nihonshi* (Great history of Japan) compiled by the Mito-*han* during the Edo period. Both the Kokugaku school and the *Dai nihonshi* presupposed Japan's unbroken existence since ancient times. As exemplified by this evidence, the method of grasping and understanding the past as diachronic history has been in use in documents in the Japanese language from very early times.

Even today, it appears that Japanese historians are expected to write a history of their specialty country/region after undergoing plentiful experiences, and acquiring a large amount of knowledge as they mature—and this is none other than diachronic history.

It is in historians' nature to ask why changes come about. In the new world history, however, I dare to propose that this method of historical understanding should be partially sealed off. For the two reasons that are presented below, any serial historical description is liable to become a specific country/region–centric history.

The prime characteristic of diachronic history is its practice to portray the history of a specific space or group of people along a time sequence. Diachronic history comes into existence when the history of a specific space or group of people is separated from the past of other spaces/groups and understood to evolve, independent of others, along a linear time sequence. This type of portrayal of history is also called a "diachronic history." In this diachronic history, a specific geographic space or group of people becomes the center of description. One should only recall such examples as British history, Chinese history, and "European" history to understand what this diachronic history is all about. And this diachronic history oftentimes leads to, say, British-centric, Sino-centric, and Euro-centric historical descriptions.

The second characteristic of diachronic history is that it always presupposes the existence of some concrete presence, be it a geographical space, a group of people, or certain things. In order for diachronic history to be viable, it has to be supposed that a certain geographical space, a certain group of people, or a certain thing actually existed for a certain period of time. This is because you cannot record the history of something that does not exist or something that is indescribable. "Europe" as a concept is provided with its own substantiality by its own history. A chronological recording of the history of "Europe" is attempted because it is considered that "Europe" does exist. Thus, European history is an important device to substantiate "Europe" as a concept. The Islam-centric historical view and the Japan-centric historical view also have basically similar structures.

In the new world history, it is only the world as a unit of time and space that should be understood by diachronic history. When the history of the world is recorded properly along the chronological sequence, the world becomes substantiated, allowing people to be convinced that indeed "there is one world" to which they can attribute their sense of belonging. While world history may ultimately be oriented toward this direction, it is, at present, difficult to portray the past of the entire world in the form of diachronic history. This is because it is not yet clear what the important keyword(s) should be. All of the necessary information is not at hand yet, either. If we try to draw a diachronic history of the world too hastily, we might end up with a "history of the victors," just as the present world history is. Information that is omitted from this portrayal will constitute peripheries. We should expect that the realization of a true diachronic history of the world is still a long way off.

QUEST FOR HORIZONTALLY CONNECTED HISTORY

Attaching More Weight to Relationship and Correlation

The third way to be rid of the Euro-centric historical view is to portray world history in a way that helps people comprehend that not only activities related to production, distribution, and consumption of people in "Europe" but also those of people all over the world together brought higher economic growth to certain countries in Europe than other regions. Readers may be annoyed by this roundabout statement. In a nutshell, I only wish to say that we should have a world history that makes people understand that it is the outcome of the activities of not only British people but people all over the world that helped Britain attain high economic growth in the nineteenth century. It may be said that this is also a task to clarify how the fifth value—that is, appropriate compensation and free exchange—of the aforementioned five important values was perceived in the past.

In order to accomplish this, it seems advisable to start with the concrete explanation that people all over the world have been related closely
to each other, particularly in the fields of trade and commodity distribution, and that they influenced each other, too. It should be stressed,
with the aid of concrete examples, that the history of trade is as old as
the history of humankind, and that trade was by no means started after
"Europeans" began to visit various places in the world in the sixteenth
century. It should also be explained well that the trading method of free
exchange was not an invention by Adam Smith or "Europe" and that it
was already being practiced in the Indian Ocean maritime world when
"Europeans" began to advance into this area.

For the world after the sixteenth century, which is usually regarded
to be a period characterized by the unilateral advancement of "Europeans"
into various places in the world, it should be relatively easy to show
that people all over the world were connected horizontally through the
medium of commodities, engaging in all kinds of activities and influenc-
ing each other. By so doing, it can be concretely presented that the world
was not divided between "Europe" or the West, on the one hand, and
"non-Europe" or Asia on the other, with each area engaged in economic
activities separately. When this method is applied, it is advisable to use
goods as an axis of serial historical description.

Because the field of historical research centered on commodities
has already yielded a substantial body of research results, as shown in
chapter 3, it should be possible to construct new interpretations on the
basis of the existing research. One can select several commodities that
seem appropriate, including spices, cotton fabric, silk fabric, metals such
as silver and copper, pottery, sugar, tea, coffee, opium, and slaves, and
explain stages of their production, distribution, sale, and consumption.
The purpose of this exercise is to present with concrete evidence that
countless people in the world were engaged in some phase of production through consumption of these global commodities in one way or
another.

It should be noted, though, that many of the studies in this field,
even those that dealt with such global commodities as sugar and tea,

have often been analyzed and explained on the basis of the unconditional premise of the presence of such frameworks as "Europe," "non-Europe," or "Asia." Also, the mainstream among them were examinations from national historical or economic historical viewpoints, such as how effective these global commodities have been for, say, British economic growth. Thus, the situation today is far from ready as far as materials for description of a new world history is concerned.

What is needed first is to multilaterally and comprehensively organize basic data on where, how, and how much a certain commodity was produced, transported, distributed, and consumed, bringing the entire world into perspective, including Eurasia-Africa, the Americas, and Oceania, instead of in the context of a single country history or bilateral relations. How much of this particular commodity had been transported from where to where also constitutes important data. How political authorities were involved in each of the production, transportation, distribution, and consumption stages should also be clarified in order to understand permeation of the concept of free exchange and its background. This will be a far more difficult task than it appears. Nevertheless, it is imperative to somehow obtain reasonably accurate data. Once data become available, it becomes possible to persuasively describe how production, transportation, distribution, and consumption of that particular commodity resulted in changes in social order, political systems, and day-to-day life of groups of people in various places in the world.

There is no center in the network composed of people who are involved in a commodity in various phases and stages, nor is there a need to search for it. It will be sufficient, instead, to portray that each person in the network played his/her own role in his/her own post and explain how this network as a whole affected the social order and political systems of the participating groups of people.

Incidentally, we have often treated countries like Britain and Japan as if they were persons with their own personalities when we describe and understand world history. For instance, in the textbook *Shōsetsu sekaishi B* (Detailed account of world history B) published by Tokyo's

Yamakawa Shuppansha, which has been adopted by the largest number of high schools in Japan, we often encounter sentences that make countries subjects, including: "After the Amboyna massacre, Britain devoted its energy to colonial management of India, actively engaging in trade with Madras, Bombay, and Calcutta as bases. Through three wars against the Netherlands, Britain attained supremacy in world trade toward the end of the seventeenth century," and "The Netherlands (United Provinces in those days) attained supremacy over Britain through the Amboyna massacre in 1623 and subsequently engaged in territorial acquisitions."[*32]

In the world history centered on the axis of goods that I propose here, it would be prudent to stay away from these expressions. The intentions and behavior of merchants, traders, and producers and consumers of goods did not necessarily coincide with the will of the states. If someone is compelled to discuss production and distribution of goods in conjunction with a state's trends, then I am afraid that person is entrapped by the framework of the present world history, which is made of numerous national histories bound together. At least until the nineteenth century, when the nation-state emerged as a solid actor, efforts should be made to make descriptions of networks of people who were engaged in a commodity's production, transportation, distribution, and consumption all over the world and the realities of people's activities in various phases understandable without making readers constantly conscious of the presence of the "state" in them.

To Relativize Interpretations

The portrayal of history differs according to the position of the person who interprets and understands the past. Therefore, interpretations in the new world history of an individual historical incident should be different from those in conventional world history. Let us dwell on this point by taking up the Industrial Revolution as an example.

[*32] Satō Tsugitaka, et al., *Shōsetsu sekaishi B* [Detailed account of world history B] (Tokyo: Yamakawa Shuppansha, 2007), 212–213.

Conventional world history pays special attention to cotton fabric and sugar among the global commodities and explains that Britain marketed these commodities efficiently via the so-called triangular trade to become the central player in world trade as the standard-bearer of free trade. In this portrayal, the transition of international trade and economic policies of such "European" countries as France and Germany, which were rivals to Britain, are hardly referred to. Thus, it would be difficult to find out—at least on the high school textbook level—what kind of trade and economic policies these European countries took, what commonalities and differences were found between their policies and British policies, or how British policies interacted with policies of these non-British countries and what outcomes came about as the result.

Nevertheless, British economic development during this era has been narrated and understood to be almost directly linked to that of "Europe." And the next thing you know is that France and Germany participated in the enterprise of the so-called division of the world as members of the "European powers." Even the Netherlands, a minor power that had to start over with a clean slate toward the end of the eighteenth century, came to be recognized as one of the world powers. It would have been impossible to reach these interpretations unless it had been assumed in the first place that "Europe" was at the center of the world and all the countries that belonged to "Europe" took concerted actions. In any event, the above is a typical view in the present world history where a state is the subject of narration.

How, then, would the new world history interpret the above same developments? It is undeniable that high economic growth and the Industrial Revolution, which had a lot to do with this high growth, commenced in the British Isles in the nineteenth century. But the new world history, unlike the conventional one, does not interpret that this revolution was carried out solely by residents of the British Isles. The new world history interprets, instead, that economic development and the Industrial Revolution were started in some parts of the British Isles as the result of the networking of various activities of people all over the world and complicated mutual influences among them. These influences included artisans in various locations on the Indian subcontinent who produced inexpensive and high-quality cotton fabric; consumers in the British Isles and Japan who had a taste for sleekly patterned Indian cotton cloth; plantation owners in the Americas and the Caribbean islands who needed slaves for farming; slave traders in various regions in Africa who earned various benefits from their trades; merchants from West Asia and South Asia who competed in Asian seas with merchants from western Eurasia; traders and smugglers from northwest European countries and the United States active in Asian seas as well as the western seas, including the North Sea and the Baltic Sea; and Russian and Turkic descendants in inland Eurasia who established a habit of drinking tea.

Perhaps, an English person who has a strong sense of belonging to Britain will not accept this historical interpretation. He/She may refute the interpretation, saying it was the invention of machinery by the English that made the Industrial Revolution possible. It is when history is told within the framework of British history that it is interpreted that Britain accomplished economic development and the Industrial Revolution ahead of other countries in the world. When history is told on the level of the world's people, the world should be the framework rather than Britain, which should lead to different interpretations. Even a great inventor in Britain is still a member of the global community. And it is also beyond doubt that behind his/her invention was the accumulation of knowledge and skills obtained through the engagements of people all over the world.

Readers may be convinced of this way of understanding when they remember how Japanese history is portrayed. Many of the heroes of the Meiji Restoration were from major domains in southwest Japan. People living in Kagoshima, Yamaguchi, and Kochi prefectures today must be proud of their fellow provincials. Needless to say, however, the Meiji Restoration was not accomplished by people from major domains in southwest Japan alone. It was an outcome of the accumulation of a variety of activities by people all over Japan and the mutual influences among them. And this is why we understand the Meiji Restoration in the framework of Japan. It is by no means a monopoly of people in

Kagoshima and Yamaguchi. The Industrial Revolution, too, should be treated in the same way. The Industrial Revolution and Britain's economic development were not accomplished by the English or "Europeans" alone. It was one of the phenomena created by all kinds of activities of people all over the world.

Similarly, if economic incidents in the world since the sixteenth century can be persuasively explained and presented as products of activities of people horizontally connected with each other across the world, we may be able to relativize the Euro-centric world history interpretation to a considerable degree.

TOWARD NEW INTERPRETATIONS

Permeation of the Concept of "Europe"

If the three methods that I have introduced are properly used, we should be able to present a new interpretation of world history that is significantly different from the present world history and its historical view. But, even if we thus succeed in dissolving "European" history, the problem of the concept of "Europe" still remains unsolved. It is beyond doubt that the concept of "Europe"—which demarcates certain people from others, perceives itself as an embodiment of progress, universality, and positive values, and perceives all others as "non-Europe"—as well as the worldview based on this concept had been shared and become considerably powerful among intellectuals not only in Western Europe, where Catholicism used to be dominant, but also in the predominantly Protestant northern Europe as well as Russia under the Eastern Orthodox Church by the end of the nineteenth century.

In the new world history, the process of the establishment of this concept and worldview must be described as scrupulously as possible. Instead of assuming the presence of two separate spaces, i.e. "Europe" and "non-Europe," from the beginning and following their respective footsteps, the new world history should state that a worldview which perceives that these two spaces have walked on different paths has become prepotent and has greatly influenced the real trends of the world. In this sense, it is extremely important to clarify how the concept of "Europe" has been formed.

This dichotomous worldview of "Europe" vs. "non-Europe" must have been a serious challenge not only to non-western Eurasian regions but also to the worldview and the social mechanism based on this worldview that had been prevalent in western Eurasia itself. While, up to the time when the concept of "Europe" was accepted and became influential, many in western Eurasia had accepted the worldview preached by the Christian church, this new view on humankind and the world pressured significant change in the traditional worldview. The "European" worldview was powerful enough to destroy the traditional social order and the political system that ensured this order, both of which were supported by the church. It can be said that this was one of the causes of political unrest and revolutions in various regions in western Eurasia in the eighteenth and nineteenth centuries.

It is worth noting that many of the worldviews that had existed in regions other than northwestern Europe were confined to people in certain regions and hardly went beyond those to spread to other groups of people. A worldview often has strong relations with social order based on the legitimacy of government and religion and, therefore, an alien worldview would not be readily accepted by a society with different logics of governance and social order.

Nevertheless, the new worldview centered on "Europe" that originated in northwestern Europe went beyond the boundary of Europe as a geographical space to spread globally. It began to have considerable influence in "non-Europe," although the degree of influence differed by region. The Euro-centric historical view prevalent in Japan, which I have made an issue of in this book, is a good example of this phenomenon.

Why, then, was the "Europe" vs. "non-Europe" worldview accepted widely, transcending differences of groups of peoples? This is the most fundamental question over which all historians have to put their heads together to come up with a convincing explanation. I am not prepared to answer this question to the satisfaction of readers. For the time being, I wish to search for the answer by deepening my consideration of concrete aspects of modernization in Japan and various regions in eastern Eurasia.

Presence of Science

Nonetheless, even at this point, I can offer a partial answer. And it is the presence of science (be it human or natural sciences), because science endorsed this worldview and persuasively presented a way to understand human beings and the world in place of Christianity.

In the nineteenth century, means of transportation and communication made tremendous advancements due, mainly, to scientific inventions in northwest Europe and the United States. Consequently, the concept of "Europe" and the values, institutions, technologies, and knowledge accompanying this concept rapidly diffused to the entire world. In the process, "non-Europeans" were exposed to powerful battleships and weapons, high-quality yet inexpensive products mass produced by machines, and convenient electric-powered instruments that were developed one after another. The "non-Europeans" were told that it was the knowledge of "Europeans" and science that had led to these products. They were also told that science advanced day by day. When, furthermore, "non-Europeans" were made to understand the theories of natural sciences, which were mathematically accurate and persuasive, I suspect many had to concede the superiority of "Europe" in these areas and move toward adopting the worldview and many values of "Europe" (be it human or natural sciences).

However, I must hastily add two notes of caution. First, as it becomes obvious when one studies Japan from the end of the shogunate through the Meiji era, that the technologies, knowledge, and mechanisms of politics and economy of "Europe" were not adopted unmodified by non-European regions of the world. Each society still utilized their already existing similar mechanisms and added partial improvements and alterations to them, using the "European" model as a reference.

And the situation was no different in other geographically European countries.

For instance, a mechanism for education and research called a "university" was prepared in various places in the world from the eighteenth to twentieth centuries. Even though they may all share the same name of "university," the mechanism's organization, financial setup, and management varied greatly from region to region. While, for instance, almost all universities in France are state run, there is no university run by the federal government in the United States. In Japanese universities, a faculty council composed of professors of a faculty is responsible for the entire departmental management and is empowered to elect the faculty dean and president of the university. But leading universities in the United States and France have no equivalent organ; in those countries, university presidents and faculty deans are usually appointed by advisory committees. The chief executive of a Chinese university is oftentimes a party cadre of the Communist Party. There is no ultimate model for an ideal university.

Second, not all the regions in the world have become "Europeanized." As exemplified by groups of people in Africa and Oceania, there were people who did not find the values and institutions of "Europe" particularly attractive, and there were others whose social systems made it difficult to adopt "European" values and institutions. While the outspread of the concept of "Europe" was a rather unusual phenomenon in world history in the sense that it profoundly impacted groups of people on a global scale, it also can be said to have followed the principle of cultural exchange that had been common in the hitherto world, seeing as groups of people in various places either adopted these values and institutions of their own will or did not adopt them. I wish to stress here that, among countries that are regarded to be "non-Europe," Japan very actively adopted the concept of "Europe" and its worldview.

We should also pay attention to the self-consciousness of people in "Europe" after the nineteenth century when they demarcated themselves from others and became convinced of their superiority over others. Those people believed that they were on the cutting edge of human history and took it on as their mission to teach their universal values to people in "non-Europe" and bring them up to their own level. This is what has been referred to as *mission civilisatrice* (civilizing mission). The northwestern European countries in the nineteenth to early twentieth centuries were endowed with the military might and economic power to convey the values of "Europe" with which they identified themselves to those who were not willing to accept them by, occasionally, imposing them on these people. It should be understood that military control and colonization were the extreme expression of this will of people in "Europe."

Distance from Nationalism

As I declared at the outset of this chapter, in order to realize a world history of the global community, all effort should be concentrated first in renovating the understanding of "European" history up to the first half of the nineteenth century. Once it becomes clear that "Europe" was a kind of ideology and that it did not experience its own unique past, separated from others, the portrayal of world history from the latter half of the nineteenth century up to the present should change fundamentally.

That being said, the closer the portrayal gets to the present time, the more difficult it will become to portray a world history of the global community. Memories of conflicts between sovereign nation-states in various places in the world still remain fresh in people's minds. In the age of the nation-state, a state's history is a common heritage of the nation. Many of the people of the countries that attained independence from colonial rulers could not easily forgive the tyrannies of their former colonizers. They may find it premature to speak of "one world." And this is perfectly understandable as coming from those who have a strong sense of belonging to a nation-state.

Nevertheless, living in today's world, we can no longer accept the nation-state as holy writ and respect its stance alone. We must continue to cherish our sense of belonging to our state, but, at the same time, we must also nurture our awareness as global citizens who share a common interest as dwellers of the earth. The important thing is to strike a balance between the two.

In the new world history, therefore, when a conflict between nations is portrayed, it will be imperative to attempt a description of the entire picture seen from a detached stance without provoking nationalism. Thus, we will probably end up explaining that nationalism and the mechanism of the nation-state became influential in many regions in the world in the nineteenth and twentieth centuries, which led to the emergence of a number of groups of people equipped with new social orders and political systems; that people obtained a new sense of belonging, identifying themselves as French nationals or German nationals, for example; and that nationalism became one of the causes of fierce confrontations among groups of people.

A few years ago, I had a chance to visit the port cities of Surat, in northwest India, and Quanzhou, in southern China. It is said that Surat and Quanzhou prospered in the seventeenth century and the thirteenth to fourteenth centuries, respectively, but both subsequently declined economically. What amazed me in both cities were the princely houses that probably had been built toward the end of the nineteenth century or in the early twentieth century. In both cities, I spotted Western decorations delicately added to local architectural styles. While some of those buildings, which were over 100 years old, were nearly in ruins because they hadn't been properly attended, there were still many others that retained their beauty and were reminiscent of glorious days gone by.

Houses in Surat (left) and Quanzhou (right). Believed to have been constructed in the early twentieth century, the houses exhibit such Western decorative characteristics as arches and balconies. (Photos taken by the author)

In the late nineteenth century through the early twentieth century, India was under Britain's colonial rule, while China was in the midst of confusion at the twilight of the Qing dynasty. According to conventional understanding of world history, those must be regarded as dark days for both countries. I was puzzled about who in those dark days had dared to build and live in those houses. Without a doubt, those houses did not belong to Western residents such as the English, because neither one of the two cities was a major stronghold for their activities in those days. It is unthinkable for the Western residents, whose numbers were limited, to require such a large number of houses. Therefore, they must have been built by prominent local residents. When I asked around and, after I came back to Japan, read related documents, I found that in Surat the houses had been constructed by exporters of cotton fabric and traders with Southeast Asia, while in Quanzhou the houses had been built by prominent overseas Chinese who had migrated to various places in Southeast Asia. This goes to show that there were a certain number of "non-Europeans" who succeeded in making a fortune from trading on the Asian seas in the late nineteenth century to the early twentieth century, at the height of imperial colonialism.

Those people were hardly highlighted by the conventional single-country history, which looks back at a country's past, attaching weight to nationalism, and world history, which is nothing but single-country histories bound together. If they were mentioned, it was usually in a negative connotation as collaborators with the Western colonialists or compradors. This was because in conventional world history, history is seen as a dichotomy between the Western rulers and India and China, the ruled.

The new world history, too, must clearly state that nationalism has greatly contributed to nation-state building and that it remains an important element of national integration. However, it is not advisable to interpret and portray world history from the standpoint of nationalism. The reality in those days must have been much more complicated than a simple confrontation between the colonial ruler and the ruled.

Colonies and Asymmetry

Allow me to share with you another personal experience. During the Edo period, Nagasaki was the only port city that was allowed to engage in foreign trade. As such, every piece of knowledge and every commodity from the "West" were brought first to this city by Dutch traders, from which they were distributed throughout Japan. Nagasaki, actually, was a port city almost solely for trade with China until the late eighteenth century, but I will not dwell on that here. In any event, the first thing that comes to people's minds when they hear the name Nagasaki is (the trade with) the Netherlands. People in Nagasaki are proud of the tie between their city and the Netherlands. Dejima, an artificial island in the bay of Nagasaki where Dutch officials and merchants were confined, has been restored to its early nineteenth-century state and is today a tourist attraction of the city.

When I visited Jakarta, Indonesia, a few years ago, I dropped by the remains of Batavia, the capital city of the Dutch East Indies. My intention was to see what had become of the city that was once called the "Queen of the Orient." A part of what used to be Batavia was barely preserved as a historical district in a corner of Jakarta. And yet, streets and canals were infested with garbage and a foul odor; buildings that must have been beautiful in their heyday were now dingy and on the verge of crumbling to the ground. The restoration of Nagasaki's Dejima flashed across my mind then, and I murmured to my colleague, a specialist in Indonesian economic history, who had kindly offered to show me around, "If they can restore this corner of Batavia to its former glory to be enjoyed by tourists, like Dejima, the area could be reinvigorated." At this suggestion, my colleague stared at me in shock and exclaimed, "That's out of the question! Indonesians would never allow such a thing. This was the stronghold of Dutch colonial rule."

I was ashamed of my inconsiderateness and lack of understanding. At the same time, his response instantly brought home to me the difficulty of narrating a world history that would satisfy everyone on earth. While the Japanese are favorably disposed toward the Netherlands as a friend who brought Western modern civilization to Japan, the Indonesians' attitude toward the Netherlands is, in contrast, generally negative. Employees of the Dutch East Indies cannot have behaved so radically different between Nagasaki and Batavia because they must have acted in both cities out of consideration for the interest of their company and of themselves. The Netherlands also must have something to say about the colonization of Indonesia in as late as the nineteenth century.

Activities of a same group of people can be viewed totally differently depending on the angle and standpoint of the viewers. This is the difficulty inherent in modern and contemporary history. The relationship between the Netherlands and Indonesians is akin to that between Japanese and Koreans. How should a world history of the global community portray the apparent asymmetry between the colonizer and the colonized? It seems there is no other way than to state the fact that the Netherlands had colonized the East Indies (present-day Indonesia) and to describe what changes thus occurred. The significance of the colonization in the context of world history should be explained carefully, without siding with one standpoint and yet paying due consideration to all. And such would be basically the same for relations between Japan and Korea and Japan and China. What needs to be done is to take up individual events and offer commentaries and, at the same time, compare these incidents and attempt to structuralize the entire world at a particular point of time.

In western Eurasia, scholars of France and Germany, two countries that fought two world wars in the twentieth century, are jointly preparing a common history textbook on modern history after World War II. A similar attempt has allegedly been started in countries on the Balkan Peninsula. These developments merit close attention as an attempt at overcoming the problem of different historical interpretations in different countries. Nonetheless, it should be quite difficult for historians from various countries to reach a conclusion that satisfies everyone if each one is not freed from the binding of his/her own country perspective. It appears that the Japan-China Joint History Research Committee and the Japan–South Korea Joint History Research Project, which are being launched based on bilateral government agreements, are not going smoothly.

As far as eastern Eurasia is concerned, historians from China, Japan, and Korea are jointly and seriously discussing how to portray modern to contemporary East Asian history on a nongovernmental basis. The success of this endeavor perhaps hinges on how free participating historians are from home country restrictions, how far they trust methods of historical studies, and how thoughtfully they interpret and discuss the past as members of the global community. If this endeavor is accomplished successfully, we may be able to glean important hints for portrayal of a new world history. I am watching developments surrounding these significant endeavors with keen expectation.

Entrapped by Expansion and Growth

Before closing this chapter, I wish to touch on the prospects of economic disparity. This is an important problem facing today's world. It should be recalled that "Europe" as a concept regarded economic expansion and growth as a positive value. Science and technology, which continues to produce one after another all manner of equipment and instruments to enhance material affluence, was also one of the positive values for "Europe." Nation-states, which were created by groups of people who placed much value on economic expansion and growth as well as on material affluence for their peoples, aimed at further expanding their economic scale and raising living standards, adopting, where appropriate, "European" political and economic mechanisms.

Yet there also existed groups of people who did not necessarily want those elements in their day-to-day lives, as well as other groups whose abrupt quest for those elements was hampered by political/economic mechanisms and social infrastructure. Consequently, these groups of people came to be inferior to those that had adopted those "European" elements in terms of economic growth and material affluence. And this is the origin of the north-south problem in today's world.

Needless to say, an evaluation of a group of people varies by what the observer values in history. Those who subscribe to the world-systems theory and try to portray history on the basis of capitalism and indices of economic development and material affluence tend to attach weight to where the center of the world economy is. Thus, if they are interested in contemporary history, they tend to stress the centricity of the United States. This does not automatically mean, however, that the United States is superior to other human societies in all aspects of life. If a different measure were applied, such as spiritual richness, the degree of happiness, social safety and a sense of security, or the burden on the environment, a different viewpoint would become viable.

Economic expansion and growth and high living standards are inextricably associated with an increase in the demand for energy. The Great East Japan Earthquake and Tsunami in 2011 brought home to us the powerlessness in the face of natural calamity of facilities constructed with the best of science. That disaster once again reminded us that what we think of as our high-quality, affluent life actually stands on a highly uncertain and fragile foundation. After the earthquake and the tsunami, nuclear power plants in Fukushima, which were supposedly constructed to generate energy to enrich our lives, raged against man. We humans have uncritically sanctioned the advancement of science and technology and found economic expansion and growth and material affluence of positive value to our lives. It is this lifestyle of ours itself that must be reexamined. Competitions among countries for economic expansion, growth, and material affluence have without a doubt become an important factor that moved world history from the nineteenth century to today. What is called for now, in my judgment, is to view world history and review its interpretation from a position detached from these values.

RENOVATION OF MODERN KNOWLEDGE

This Book's Argument

People belong to multiple organizations in their day-to-day lives. In contemporary Japan, representative organizations that people belong to include family, kinsfolk, municipalities, the state, companies, schools, alumni associations, and clubs of like-minded people. Many believe that it is important for the Japanese people to have an awareness of the state of Japan and of themselves as belonging to that state.

Ordinarily, it is believed that each one of these human groups has its own history. A family has a family history, a university has its own history, and a municipality has its history. The awareness that they share a common history strengthens comradeship among members, which, in turn, intensifies the group's unity. It is only natural for the Japanese government to request that compulsory education teach pupils and students Japanese history with an aim at instilling in future generations of Japanese an awareness of themselves as Japanese nationals.

Similarly, in order for us to become keenly aware that we are members of the global community and to heighten our sense of belonging to this earth, a history of the global community will be indispensable. But what is called for is by no means a world history comprised of histories of individual countries, such as Japan, the United States, and China, merely bound together. A history of the global community cannot be a collection of histories of various regional worlds, such as Europe and East Asia, either. While these "world histories" may be able to strengthen people's sense of belonging to their own country or region, they are useless for nurturing people's awareness of themselves as citizens of the global community. A history of the global community must be something that says that "there is one world" and which portrays the pasts of all the people in the world without failing to pay careful attention to all of them. This kind of world history must be conceived anew. This is the argument put forth in this book.

The real world today is composed of sovereign states as its basic unit. Because a state is the basic unit to which people in today's world feel a sense of belonging, it will be extremely difficult to realize a world history of the global community. Nevertheless, it is a challenge that is worth trying. When the future direction of today's world is considered in earnest, it becomes obvious that a world history of the global community is an enterprise that must be accomplished at any cost. As we continue to actively discuss the concept of a world history of the global community, it will in time grow into a powerful force and point to the future that people should aspire for.

The Islamic World as One of the "Others"

When I started studying history in graduate school, I regarded myself as a student of history of the Safavid dynasty. The Safavid dynasty ruled the areas around the Iranian Plateau in West Asia between the sixteenth and eighteenth centuries. I wrote my doctoral dissertation at Université de Paris III on the history of this dynasty's political systems in my twenties. Subsequently, my interest expanded gradually to include the cities and architecture in the region as well as the history of other regions in the Middle East, making me believe that, in the 1990s, I was studying the history of the Islamic world. I received more and more invitations to speak at universities and public lectures on not only Islamic history but also the Islamic religion and Muslims in general. And every time I was given such an opportunity, I repeatedly argued that in Japan the general understanding of the Islamic religion and its believers was misguided, that Islam is not such a rigid and fanatic religion, and that the majority of Muslims are people of sound judgment who can get along well with the Japanese people without any problem.

Nevertheless, "common knowledge" dies hard. In fact, since the September 11 attacks in the United States in 2001, the Japanese people's attitude toward Islam and Muslims has become increasingly intolerant. And this phenomenon is not confined to Japan. Talking to friends in China and Korea, not to mention Western friends, I often encountered such almost radical reactions as, "Muslims are out of the ordinary." Crestfallen over my powerlessness, I also began to wonder seriously why people's common understanding was so difficult to change. My book, *Isuramu sekai no sōzō* (Creating the notion of the Islamic world), which I published from the University of Tokyo Press in 2005, was an interim report of my quest for the answer to this question. In that book, I pointed to the problem of the concept of an "Islamic world" that had been created by "Europe" in the nineteenth century and raised an alarm over the tendency to too easily resort to the Islamic world to explain various incidents in today's world. The book received considerable attention from readers and was reviewed and introduced many times by newspapers and magazines. Unfortunately, however, the book had absolutely no impact on the way journalism in Japan narrated and explained world situations.

While I was only vaguely conscious of the root cause of the problem when I was writing that book, I feel confident now that I have a clear view of it. It is not the Islamic world alone that is the problem. The problem is our view of the entire world, which we have almost unconsciously accepted as common understanding.

Let us compare the world to a jigsaw puzzle. The Islamic world is a piece of this puzzle. It is the premise of the game that the overall design of the world is predetermined. Therefore, the color and shape of each puzzle piece cannot be altered freely. The overall design cannot be completed if the color or shape of a portion is changed. Players are free to pick up any piece and discuss its color or shape. But when that particular piece is placed on the puzzle, it has to fit into the overall design. And this is why people's view on Islam would not change no matter how tenaciously I stressed that their understanding of Islam was wrong. As long as I explain the design or color of Islam or the Islamic world piece, people understand me and say, "Oh, I see. So that was how it was, was it?" However, as soon as the piece is placed on the overall design, people's understanding of Islam goes back to the original form. This is because the overall pattern is fixed.

Renovation of Humanities and Social Sciences Knowledge

What, then, does this overall design look like? Where and how was it determined? The foundation of the overall design is the "Europe" vs. "non-Europe" worldview that had emerged clearly by the latter half of the nineteenth century. Since then, people who accepted this worldview have strenuously continued to refine its colors and patterns in various places in the world. Its basic structural outline is the dichotomous worldview that demarcates between oneself and others and believes that the progressive "Europe" or "the West" (the term often used when the importance of the United States is strongly perceived) is different from others. The nation-state system, such as France and Japan, is also based on this dichotomous worldview in the sense that states demarcate themselves from other states.

Many of the humanities and social sciences disciplines, which were established in the nineteenth century through the early twentieth century, adopted this dichotomous perspective and became theorized and systematized. In the course of such, they became equipped with methodologies for demarcation, including those for pigeonholing and analyzing information, and they have continued to reproduce knowledge in line with this dichotomous perspective to this date. While space does not permit me to dwell on this point at length, this should be easy to understand when one recalls the old-time Marxist economics and historical studies, which posited the capitalist "Europe" as having a higher rank of developmental stage and Asia, which persisted with the "Asiatic mode of production," as being backward. All the humanities, including literature, philosophy, and religious studies, as well as social sciences such as political science, economics, and sociology, have more or less tacitly presupposed this asymmetrical and dichotomous worldview as a premise of research. Many intellectuals in "non-Europe," such as those in Japan and China, have accepted this worldview and, on that basis, seriously explored the position of their country and people in this worldview.

It must be pointed out that the aggregate knowledge about the world by the humanities and social sciences, which has been produced over the past 100 years or more, tightly constrains our view on the world. It is only natural that it should be hard to change ordinary people's perception of the world. To repeat one example, the position and role of the "Islamic world" has been fixed in the humanities and social sciences body of knowledge based on the perception of the world since the nineteenth century. No matter how tenaciously I explain, the "Islamic world" as one of the "others" can never become "oneself."

What I have tried to accomplish through this book, despite my limited capacities, is to renovate the view on world history, because the view of world history is one of the important elements that has constrained our viewpoint on the world. History plays a major role when people try to understand today's world. Therefore, unless the very basis for the perception of the world that we have unconsciously accepted is changed, we will find ourselves trying to solve the problems of the contemporary world in a blind alley—which is difficult.

Some may criticize the slogan "there is one world" for being too naïve, too sentimental, and too un-academic. They may say that it would not be possible to talk about a new world history without envisioning the concrete form of the future world political regime, whether it be a world republic, a world federation, a united states of the world, or a federation of regional communities. In this book, however, I wish to confine myself to presenting the slogan and the common values that we should realize without discussing concrete political regimes of the future. This is because I expect that the future shape of the world will automatically make its appearance as the discussion of a new world history becomes increasingly active. It is my wish that this book becomes a switch to ignite the discussion.

Recently, in the fields of the humanities, a movement similar to the concept of a new world history has begun. The movement includes a scheme to compile a world literature along similar lines to a new world history, to relativize the framework of national literature, to review studies of philosophical ideas that have so far been clustered by the nation-state paradigm (e.g., Chinese philosophy, French philosophical thought, etc.), to reexamine such concepts as religion and beauty—as well as countless other new tendencies. Once these academic endeavors are united to form a massive intellectual trend, and once that trend starts producing tangible outcomes one after another, the perspectives of people all over the world will begin to change. It may be quite some time before this actually takes place. Nevertheless, I am determined to continue my walk toward this goal, hand in hand with my colleagues, without taking my eyes off of the remote future.

AFTERWORD

I t was immediately after I published *Isuramu sekai no sōzō* (Creating the notion of the Islamic world) in July 2005 that I became aware that I had to write about a new world history next. In fact, as I was writing that book, I had already become conscious of the unnaturalness of the world history that incorporates the history of the "Islamic world." In the autumn of the same year, I attended a symposium during the annual meeting of the Historical Society of Japan. I still remember well that, when I spoke with Ms. Nakanishi Sawako, a long-time acquaintance of mine who was with the Editorial Department of Iwanami Shoten Publishers at that time, I replied enthusiastically that I would be most interested in writing about world history.

Six years have already elapsed since then. It is not that I have wasted those six years. The world history that I wanted to write proved to be too tough for me to tackle. For one thing, I could not penetrate the thick wall of conventional world history with a one-point charge from the angle of Islamic world history. It brought home to me the difficulty of creating something new, while it is easy to criticize something that is already there. I somehow managed to keep my promise to Ms. Nakanishi by publishing this book, but I am fully aware that I have a long way to go to accomplish my goal of writing a new world history.

Meanwhile, I was presented with opportunities to organize two world history–related joint research projects with the help of the Grants-in-Aid for Scientific Research program of the Japan Society for the Promotion of Science as well as to participate in several other joint research and publication projects. Each one of them was a precious opportunity for me to be academically stimulated and to review and refine my thinking. Space does not allow me to introduce all of these projects, but I wish to share with readers my experiences with three projects in particular that greatly influenced me in writing this book.

First, I must mention the University of Tokyo Center for Philosophy (UTCP) led by Professors Kobayashi Yasuo and Nakajima Takahiro. The center is one of the university's Global COE (Center of Excellence) projects. Previously, I had had no contact with philosophy at all in my day-to-day life. I was exposed to a fraction of philosophical thinking and debating methods through intensive discussions that were repeatedly held in this internationally open center, making me realize problems that the disciplines of the humanities commonly face. While it makes me uneasy to wonder how much of what I learned from this experience is actually utilized in this book, it is beyond any doubt that my association with this center broadened my horizons.

Second, I wish to touch on the joint research project on Maritime Cross-Cultural Exchange in East Asia and the Formation of Japanese Traditional Culture, which I introduced in chapter 3. Led by Kojima Tsuyoshi, then associate professor at the University of Tokyo, this was a grand project that brought together a hundred and some dozens of humanities researchers engaged in studies related to China, Korea, and Japan. As one of the few non–East Asia specialists participating in the project, I was given the opportunity to glimpse the China issue; since then, I have become conscious of problems inherent in the concept of "East Asia." It was also an opportunity for me to ponder a method for a maritime world history together with my fellow participants.

Third, I am a member of the editorial committee of the Minerva World History Library sponsored by the Kyoto-based publisher Minerva Shobo. I have had chances to fervently discuss the significance and methodologies of a new world history over and over with other members of the committee, including Akita Shigeru, Mitani Hiroshi, Minamizuka Shingo, Nagahara Yōko, and Momoki Shirō. These precious and highly joyous experiences gave me many ideas, some of which are incorporated in the present volume.

In addition, I benefitted immensely from my acquaintances with Ge Zhaoguang, professor, National Institute for Advanced Humanistic Studies, Fudan University in Shanghai, and Benjamin Elman, director, East Asian Studies Program, Princeton University. I met these two professors in my role as director of the University of Tokyo's Institute for Advanced Studies on Asia when we launched an academic exchange consortium with their two institutions. Ge and Elman are both world-class scholars in East Asian history, and I learned a lot from their presentations at symposiums and occasional remarks.

I also wish to acknowledge friends and colleagues who directly helped me complete this book. Naitō Mariko, a young friend of mine with whom I became acquainted at the aforementioned UTCP, read all of my not-too-easy-to-read draft manuscripts, pointed out a lot of errors, and gave me invaluable advice. Her painstaking efforts are highly appreciated. I also benefitted from comments on my draft manuscript from Kanahara Noriko and Terada Yūki. They are not historical researchers in the narrow sense of the word but, or because so, they did not overlook dubious points which had escaped my attention. Although I was not able to adopt all of their sharp suggestions in the present volume, I am nevertheless grateful for their earnest advice. At Iwanami Shoten, Naganuma Kōichi was put in charge of editing this book after Nakanishi was transferred to another department. I was helped immensely by his accurate judgment, shrewd advice, and prompt execution.

Although space does not permit me to mention by name each and every one of the other numerous friends, colleagues, and associates who gave me countless suggestions and advice, I would like to express my heartfelt gratitude to them, including my colleagues at the Institute for Advanced Studies on Asia, the University of Tokyo, and associates in the grant-in-aid research project on "Eurasia in the Modern Period: Towards a New World History" of the Japan Society for the Promotion of Science.

It is my wish that this book induce vigorous discussions about views on world history, historical research methods, and our perceptions of world history.

September 2011
Haneda Masashi

195

BIBLIOGRAPHY

Asahi Shimbun. Morning edition, January 28, 2009.

Braudel, Fernand. *La Méditerranée et le Monde Méditerranéen a l'époque de Philippe II* [*The Mediterranean and the Mediterranean World in the Age of Philip II*]. Paris: Armand Colin, 1949.

Chizuka, Tadami. *Shigaku gairon* [Introduction to historical studies]. Tokyo: University of Tokyo Press, 2010.

Diamond, Jared. *Guns, Germs, and Steel: The Fates of Human Societies*. New York: W. W. Norton, 1997.

Frank, Andre. *Reorient: Global Economy in the Asian Age*. Berkeley: University of California Press, 1998.

Haneda, Masashi. *Isuramu sekai no sōzō* [Creating the notion of the Islamic world]. Tokyo: University of Tokyo Press, 2005.

———. "Isuramu sekai to atarashii sekaishi" [The Islamic world and new world history], *Gurōbaru hisutorī no chōsen* [Challenge of global history], Mizushima Tsukasa, ed. Tokyo: Yamakawa Shuppansha, 2008.

Kanehara, Nobukatsu. *Senryaku gaikō genron* [Principles of strategic diplomacy]. Tokyo: Nippon Keizai Shinbun Shuppansha, 2011.

Kawakita, Minoru. *Satō no sekaishi* [World history of sugar]. Tokyo: Iwanami Shoten, 1996.

Kubodera, Kōichi. *Tōyōgaku kotohajime: Naka Michiyo to sono jidai* [Beginning of oriental studies: Naka Michiyo and his time]. Tokyo: Heibonsha, 2009.

Le Quintrec, Guillaume. *Histoire 2de: livre de l'élève*. Paris: Nathan, 2001.

———. *Histoire, terminale L-ES*. Paris: Nathan, 2004.

Marks, Robert B. *The Origins of the Modern World*, 2nd edition. Lanham: Rowman & Littlefield, 2007.

Marseille, Jacques. *Marseille: Histoire, 1ère, Bac L, ES*. Paris: Nathan, 2003.

Michelet, Jules. *Le peuple*, 5e édition. Paris: Calmann-Lévy, 1877.

Minamizuka, Shingo. *Sekaishi nante iranai?* [We don't need world history, do we?]. Tokyo: Iwanami Shoten, 2007.

Ministry of Education, Culture, Sports, Science and Technology's Curriculum Guideline. http://www.mext.go.jp/component/a_menu/education/micro_detail/__icsFiles/afieldfile/2011/03/30/1304427_002.pdf.

Ministry of Education, Science and Culture's Curriculum Guideline.
1947: https://www.nier.go.jp/guideline/s22ejs3/chap1.htm.
1951: https://www.nier.go.jp/guideline/s26jhs3/chap2.htm.
1956: https://www.nier.go.jp/guideline/s31hs/chap5.htm.
1960: https://www.nier.go.jp/guideline/s35h/chap2-2.htm.
1970: https://www.nier.go.jp/guideline/s45h/chap2-2.htm

Miyazaki, Ichisada. Afterword to *Miyazaki Ichisada zenshū 2: Tōyōshi* [Complete works of Miyazaki Ichisada 2: Oriental history]. Tokyo: Iwanami Shoten, 1992.

———. Foreword to *Ajia rekishi kenkyū nyūmon*, dai 1-kan [Introduction to Asian historiographical studies, vol. 1], Shimada Kenji, ed. Kyoto: Dohosha Shuppan, 1983.

Mizushima, Tsukasa. *Gurōbaru hisutorī nyūmon* [Introduction to global history]. Tokyo: Yamakawa Shuppansha, 2010.

Ogata, Isamu, et al. *Sekaishi B* [World history B]. Tokyo: Tokyo Shoseki, 2007.

Satō, Tsugitaka, et al. *Shōsetsu sekaishi B* [Detailed account of world history B]. Tokyo: Yamakawa Shuppansha, 2007.

"Sekai no rekishi" Henshū Iinkai, ed. *Mō ichido yomu Yamakawa sekaishi* [Yamakawa's world history revisited]. Tokyo: Yamakawa Shuppansha, 2009.

Shibata, Michio, et al. *Shinsekaishi* [New World History]. Tokyo: Yamakawa Shuppan, 2009.

Uehara, Senroku, et al. ed. *Nihon kokumin no sekaishi* [World history for the Japanese people]. Tokyo: Iwanami Shoten, 1960.

Wang, Side, ed. *Shijie tongshi* [Overview of world history], 2nd edition. Shanghai: East China Normal University Press, 2009.

Further Readings

Belich, James, et al. *The Prospect of Global History*. Oxford: Oxford University Press, 2016.

The Cambridge World History, 7 vols. Cambridge: Cambridge University Press, 2015.

Conrad, Sebastian. *What Is Global History?* Princeton: Princeton University Press, 2016.

Haneda, Masashi. "A New Global History and Regional Histories," Benjamin Elman and Chao-Hui Jenny Liu, eds., *The 'Global' and the 'Local' in Early Modern and Modern East Asia*. Leiden: Brill, 2017: 52–65.

——. "Japanese Perspective on Global History," *Asian Review of World Histories*, 3, no. 2, 2015: 219–234.

——."Le Japon et la mer," Christian Buchet and Gerard Le Bouedec, eds. *La mer dans l'histoire*, vol. 3. Suffolk: Boydell Press, 2017: 564–579.

Hunt, Lynn. *Writing History in the Global Era*. New York: Norton, 2014.

Northrop, Douglas, ed. *A Companion to World History*. Oxford: Wiley-Blackwell, 2012.

Olstein, Diego. *Thinking History Globally*. New York: Palgrave Macmillan, 2014.

Osterhammel, Jürgen. *The Transformation of the World: A Global History of the Nineteenth Century*. Princeton: Princeton University Press, 2014.

AUTHOR'S PROFILE

Haneda Masashi is executive vice president of the University of Tokyo and a professor of the Institute for Advanced Studies on Asia (IASA) at the University of Tokyo, and his field of specialty is global and world history. Born in 1953, Haneda earned his B.A. and M.A. at Kyoto University, and Doctorat de troisième cycle (Ph.D.) at Université de Paris III in 1983. He served as associate professor at the Faculty of Humanities, Tachibana Women's College (present-day Kyoto Tachibana University), visiting scholar at CNRS (France) and the University of Cambridge, associate professor at IASA in 1989, professor at IASA in 1997, director of IASA 2009–12, and vice president of the University of Tokyo 2012–15 before assuming his current position. He is the author of *Le chāh et les Qizilbāš* (K. Schwarz, 1987), and editor of *Islamic Urban Studies* (Kegan Paul, 1994). His publications in the Japanese language include *Isuramu sekai no sōzō* [Creating the notion of the Islamic world] (University of Tokyo Press, 2005); *Iwanami Isuramu jiten* [Iwanami dictionary of Islam] (editor, Iwanami Shoten, 2002); *Mosuku ga kataru Isuramushi* [Islamic history as told by mosques] (Chuokoronsha, 1994); and *Higashi Indo Gaisha to Ajia no umi* [East India Companies and Asian water] (Kodansha, 2007).

ABOUT THE TRANSLATOR

Trained in international relations and economics, Noda Makito has translated numerous books and treatises, including *Fifteen Lectures on Showa Japan* (co-translated with Paul Narum) and *The Self-Defense Forces and Postwar Politics in Japan*, which were published as part of the Japan Library.

（英文版）新しい世界史へ
Toward Creation of a New World History

2018年3月27日　第1刷発行

著　者　　羽田　正
訳　者　　野田　牧人
発行所　　一般財団法人出版文化産業振興財団
　　　　　〒101-0051　東京都千代田区神田神保町3-12-3
　　　　　電話　03-5211-7282 ㈹
　　　　　ホームページ　http://www.jpic.or.jp/

印刷・製本所　大日本印刷株式会社